Microsoft PowerPoint 2023 From Zero to Hero

How to Become a Master of Microsoft PowerPoint in Less Than 7 Minutes a Day with the Most Updated Guide (Step-By-Step Tutorial) + Bonus: The 10 Most Essential Formulas Requested by any Company

© Copyright 2022 by - All rights reserved.

This document is geared towards providing exact and reliable information in regard to the topic and issue covered. The publication is sold with the idea that the publisher is not required to render accounting, officially permitted, or otherwise, qualified services. If advice is necessary, legal or professional, a practiced individual in the profession should be ordered.

From a Declaration of Principles which was accepted and approved equally by a Committee of the American Bar Association and a Committee of Publishers and Associations.

In no way is it legal to reproduce, duplicate, or transmit any part of this document in either electronic means or in printed format. Recording of this publication is strictly prohibited and any storage of this document is not allowed unless with written permission from the publisher. All rights reserved.

The information provided herein is stated to be truthful and consistent, in that any liability, in terms of inattention or otherwise, by any usage or abuse of any policies, processes, or directions contained within is the solitary and utter responsibility of the recipient reader. Under no circumstances will any legal responsibility or blame be held against the publisher for any reparation, damages, or monetary loss due to the information herein, either directly or indirectly.

Respective authors own all copyrights not held by the publisher.

The information herein is offered for informational purposes solely and is universal as so. The presentation of the information is without contract or any type of guarantee assurance.

The trademarks that are used are without any consent, and the publication of the trademark is without permission or backing by the trademark owner. All trademarks and brands within this book are for clarifying purposes only and are the owned by the owners themselves, not affiliated with this document.

Table of Contents

Introduction

Chapter 1: Getting Started With PowerPoint
- 1.1 Start PowerPoint
- 1.2 Work in the PowerPoint User Interface
- 1.3 Identify App Window Elements
- 1.4 Work with the Ribbon & Status Bar

Chapter 2: Managing Presentations
- 2.1 Create Presentations
- 2.2 Display Different Views of Presentations
- 2.3 Display & Edit Presentation Properties
- 2.4 Save & Close Presentations

Chapter 3: Manage & Create Slides
- 3.1 Add & Remove Slides
- 3.2 Insert New Slides
- 3.3 Divide Presentations Into Sections
- 3.4 Rearrange Slides & Sections
- 3.5 Change Slide Backgrounds

Chapter 4: Manage & Insert Text On Slides
- 4.1 Enter Text On Slides
- 4.2 Move, Copy & Delete Text
- 4.3 Format Characters & Paragraphs

Chapter 5: Insert & Manage Images & Graphics
5.1 Insert, Move & Resize Pictures
5.2 Edit & Format Pictures
5.3 Create Charts
Chapter 6: Finalize Presentation
6.1 Configure Slides For Presentation Or Printing
6.2 Print Presentations & Handouts
6.3 10 Essential Formulas Requested by a Company
Conclusion

Introduction

PowerPoint, which is included in the most recent desktop productivity package, offers a comprehensive range of tools for generating presentations. This section of the book will introduce target consumers to this presentation software, highlighting new capabilities and explaining how to use it to build and work with visually appealing, highly professional presentations. These chapters will teach you all you need to be able to begin using PowerPoint efficiently at home, at business, and for certification.

PowerPoint is part of Microsoft Office, which also contains Word, Excel, and Outlook.

PowerPoint is a presentation application and one of my favorite programs. It's intended to be used in conjunction with a big Tv or a projector to showcase presentations that will dazzle your members of the audience and instantly help influence them to your viewpoint, whether you're trying to sell real estate on Mars, Las Vegas Raiders season tickets or a new tax increase during an election year. If you've ever used a flip chart, you'll enjoy PowerPoint.

PowerPoint presentations may be an effective method to deliver information in bite-sized chunks. Bullet points, photos, tables, charts, and business diagrams may all be included on individual slides. Themes that have been professionally developed aesthetically improve your message and offer a professional, cohesive look.

The user interface refers to the aspects that influence the look of PowerPoint and how you interface with it when creating presentations. Some user interface aspects are just ornamental, such as the color scheme. Others, such as menus, toolbars and buttons, are useful. The default PowerPoint setup and functionality are based on how the majority of users use the software. You may change the appearance and functionality of user interface components to fit your tastes and working style.

Chapter 1: Getting Started With PowerPoint

PowerPoint presentations may be an effective method to deliver information in bite-sized chunks. Bullet points, photos, tables, charts, and business diagrams may all be included on individual slides. Themes that have been professionally developed aesthetically improve your message and offer a professional, cohesive look.

The user interface refers to the aspects that influence the look of PowerPoint and how you interface with it when creating presentations. Some user interface aspects are just ornamental, such as the color scheme. Others, such as menus, toolbars and buttons, are useful. The default PowerPoint setup and functionality are based on how the majority of users use the software. You may change the appearance and functionality of user interface components to fit your tastes and working style.

This chapter walks you through launching PowerPoint, using the PowerPoint user experience, and controlling Office and application settings.

1.1 Start PowerPoint

The method you use to launch PowerPoint 2016 is determined by the computer system on your computer. As an example:

- PowerPoint may be launched via the Start menu, an All Apps tab, the taskbar, or the Start screen search box in Windows 10.
- In Windows 8, users may launch PowerPoint from the Apps panel or the search results on the Start screen.
- PowerPoint may be launched from a Start menu, the All Applications menu or the Start menu search engine results in Windows 7.

You may also have a PowerPoint shortcut on your desktops or on a Windows taskbar.

The PowerPoint Start button occurs when you launch PowerPoint without first launching a presentation. The Start button is a mix of the Backstage view's Open and New pages. It shows current file links in the left pane and new file designs on the right side of the window.

1.2 Work in the PowerPoint User Interface

The PowerPoint user experience gives you easy access to all of the features you need to create a complex presentation suited to your audience's demands. PowerPoint 2023 allows you to perform the following (and a lot more):

- Create, format, import, and modify slide material such as text, photos, charts, tables, symbols, shapes, SmartArt diagrams, equations, recordings of audio and video and so on.
- Record screenshots, screencasts, and audio recordings.
- Divide and organize slides into parts.
- Animate slide content and transitions between slides; control the shape, timing, and sound of animations.
- Keep track of the speaker notes for every slide.

- Manage content layout by generating bespoke masters; accurately align slide components using layout and Smart Guides.
- Design, practice, deliver, and record unique slide displays.
- Presentations may be saved, exported, and distributed in a number of formats.
- Create OneNote notebook notes that connect to particular slide material.

When you open a presentation, it appears in an app window with all of the tools you have to add and edit information.

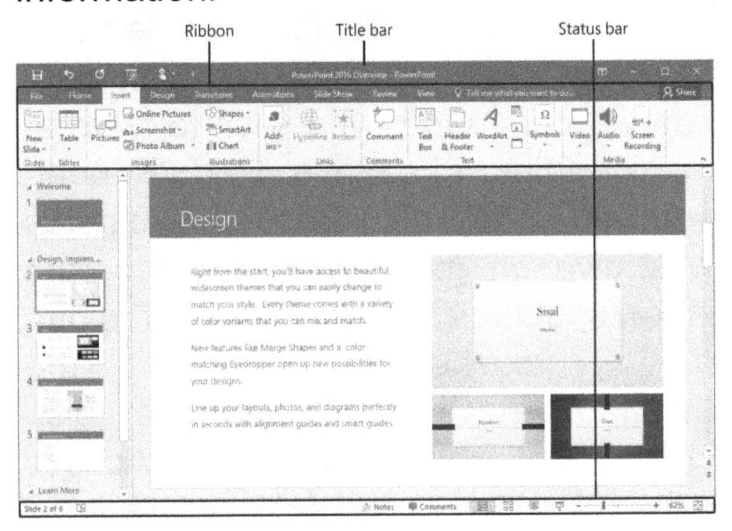

1.3 Identify App Window Elements

The items covered in this section are found in the PowerPoint program window. Commands for commonly performed operations are easily accessible, as are those for seldom performed jobs.

Title bar

This bar at the head of an app window shows the current file's name, identifies the program and gives options for modifying the ribbon, app window, and content.

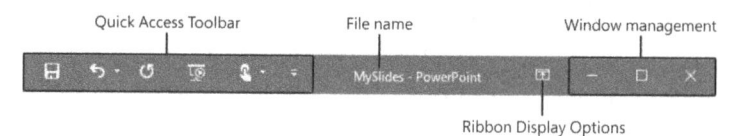

The Instant Access Toolbar at a left end of a title bar may be configured to contain whatever commands you wish to have at your fingertips. The Save, Redo/Repeat, Undo, and Start With Beginning buttons are shown on the PowerPoint program window's default Quick Access Toolbar. On a touchscreen display, the Touch/Mouse Control button is also included in the standard Quick Access Toolbar.

You may move the Instant Access Toolbar and configure it to contain any command you wish to have quick access to.

In all Office programs, four keys at the correct side of a title bar perform the same duties. You may minimize the window momentarily, change its size with the Restore Maximize/Down button, and end the current presentation or leave the program entirely by using the Close button.

Ribbon

The ribbon is seen underneath the title bar. For convenience, the commands you'll need while dealing with a slideshow are grouped together in one convenient spot.

A row of tabs runs from across the top of the ribbon. When you click a tab, you'll see a list of commands organized into categories.

The Backstage view, which you access by choosing the File tab at the left end of the ribbon, collects commands relevant to controlling PowerPoint and slideshows (rather than presentation content). The Backstage view's commands are grouped on named sheets, which you may access by selecting the tabs in a colored left pane. By selecting the Back arrow positioned above the page tabs, you may re-display the presentations and the ribbon.

You manage files and app settings in the Backstage view

The other tabs of a ribbon include buttons that indicate commands related to interacting with presentation material. The most commonly used commands are located on the Main screen, which would be enabled by default.

When you choose a visual element on a slide, such as a photo, table, or chart, one or even more tool tabs may appear at the right end of the ribbon, making actions relating to that particular item readily available. When the necessary item is chosen, tool tabs become accessible.

Buttons indicating commands are arranged into designated groups on each tab. You may click on any button to see a

ScreenTip with the command name, an explanation of its purpose, and a keyboard alternative (if it has one).

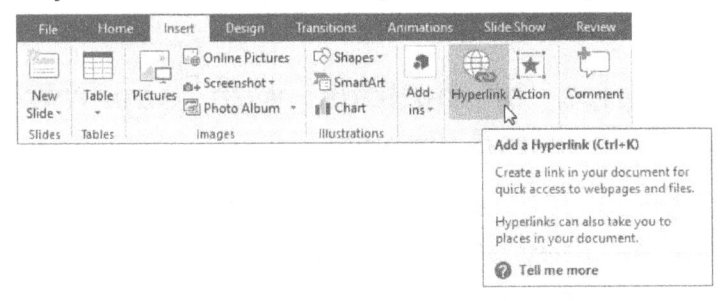

ScreenTips can include the command name, keyboard shortcut, and description

Some buttons have an arrow that is either incorporated with or independent from the button. To see whether a start button and its arrows are merged, point to a button and press it. When both the buttons and their arrows are colored, pressing the button brings up choices for fine-tuning the button's function. When you point to a button or arrow that is just shaded, clicking it performs its default function or applies the existing default formatting. The action is carried out by clicking an arrow and then selecting an action. Clicking an arrow and then a formatting choice applies the style and makes it the button's default.

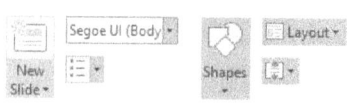

Examples of buttons with separate and integrated arrows

When a format option includes several options, they are often shown as a gallery of pictures called thumbnails that offer a visual display of each option. When you click on a picture in a collection, the Live View feature displays a preview of the current content if you select the thumbnail to perform the related formatting. When there are more thumbnails in a gallery than can be displayed in the remaining ribbon area, you may display additional material by clicking the scrolling arrow or the More button situated on the gallery's right border.

Related but less frequent instructions are not represented by a series of buttons. Instead, they're accessible in a dialogue box or window, which you may access by selecting the dialogue box launcher in the group's lower-right corner.

Status bar

The status bar at the bottom of an app window shows details about the current show and gives access to specific PowerPoint capabilities. You have the ability to choose which data and tools display in the status bar. Some status bar items, like Document Updates Available, show only when that condition is met.

At the right-hand side of the status bar are the Notes and Comments icons, the View Shortcuts toolbar, the Zoom Slider tool, and the Zoom button. These tools make it simple to change the way presentation material is shown.

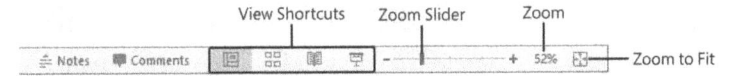

1.4 Work with the Ribbon & Status Bar

The ribbon's objective is to make dealing with presentation material as simple as possible. The ribbon is flexible, which means that its buttons adjust to the available area as its width varies. As a consequence, a button may be big or tiny, have or lack a name, or even transform into an item in a list.

When there is enough horizontal space, for example, the icons on a View tab of a PowerPoint program window are stretched out, allowing you to study the commands accessible in each group.

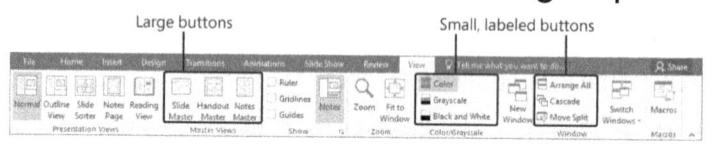

When the horizontal space given to the ribbon is reduced, little button labels vanish, and whole groups of buttons may disappear behind a single button that symbolizes the entire group. When you click the group button, a list of the instructions accessible in that group appears.

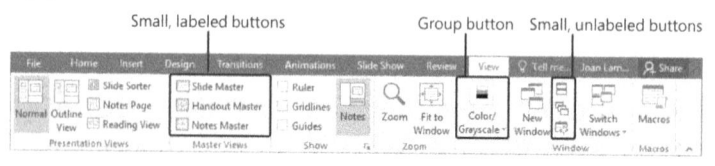

A scroll arrow emerges at the right end of the ribbon when it gets too thin to show all of the groupings. The hidden groups are seen when you click the scroll arrow.

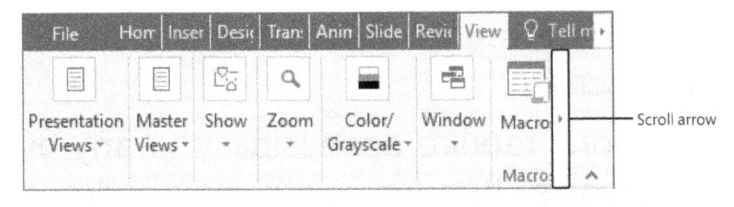

[Ribbon screenshot showing tabs: File, Home, Insert, Design, Transitions, Animations, Slide, Review, View, Tell me. Buttons: Presentation Views, Master Views, Show, Zoom, Color/Grayscale, Window, Macros. Label: Scroll arrow]

The ribbon width is determined by three factors:

• Window size The ribbon has the greatest space when the app window is maximized.

• Display resolution The dimension of your display panel is given in pixels wide by pixels high. The more information that can fit on one screen, the higher the screen resolution. Your screen resolution settings are determined by the display adapter in your computer as well as the monitor. The most common screen resolutions vary from 800 600 to 2560 1440. (and some are larger). The bigger the pixels number wide (the first value), the more buttons may be displayed on the ribbon.

• The screen display magnification When the screen magnification option in Windows is changed, text and user interface components become bigger and hence more readable, but fewer items fit on the screen.

If you don't require accessibility to any of the ribbon's buttons, you may hide it altogether or conceal it so that just its tabs are displayed. (When operating on a smaller screen, this is a wonderful technique to acquire vertical space.) The ribbon may then be momentarily re-displayed to press a button or continuously re-displayed if you have to click numerous buttons.

If you're working on a touchscreen device, you may enable Touch mode, which adds additional space between ribbon buttons and the status bar. (This has no effect on the layout of dialogue boxes or panels.) The additional space is meant to reduce the likelihood of your finger mistakenly touching the incorrect button.

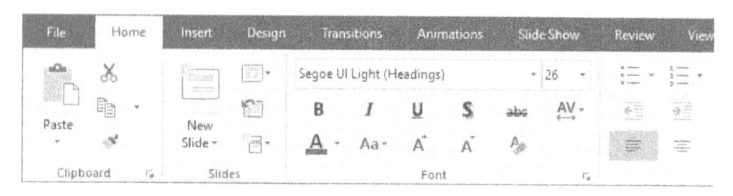

In Touch mode, the same instructions are accessible; however, they are often obscured behind group buttons.

A Quick Access Toolbar allows you to switch from mouse mode and Touch mode (the conventional desktop programs user interface). Switching to Touch mode in any of the key Office programs (Access, Outlook, Excel, PowerPoint, and Word) activates it in all of them.

To maximize the app window

Perform any one of the following:

• Select the Maximize option.

• Click a title bar twice.

• Drag the non-maximized window's edges.

Move the window to a top of a screen by dragging it. (The dragged window maximizes when the cursor reaches the top of a screen.)

To change the screen resolution

Perform any of the following:

- Right-click on the Windows 10 desktops and choose Display settings. Click the Various display options link

at the bottom of the Settings window's Display pane.
- From the Windows 7 desktop or Windows 8, choose Screen resolution.
- In Windows Search, type screen resolution, and then select Change screen resolution in search results.
- Select Display Control Panel, then click Customize resolution.
- Click or drag to pick the desired screen resolution, then select Apply or OK. Windows show a sample of the screen resolution you've chosen.
- In the notice box that opens, click Keep changes if you like the modification. If you do not, the screen resolution will return to its prior preset.

To completely hide the ribbon

Click on the Ribbon Display Settings icon near the right-hand side of a title bar.

Ribbon Display Options

Auto-hide Ribbon
Hide the Ribbon. Click at the top of the application to show it.

Show Tabs
Show Ribbon tabs only. Click a tab to show the commands.

Show Tabs and Commands
Show Ribbon tabs and commands all the time.

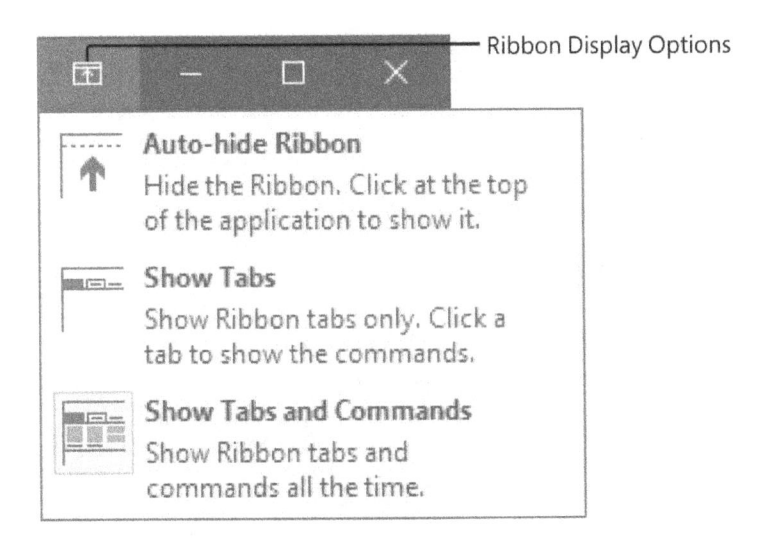

Select Auto-hide Ribbon from the Ribbon Appearance Options menu.

Just show the ribbon tabs 1.

Perform any of the following:

- Double-click the name of any active tab.
- In the program window's upper-right corner, select the Ribbon Presentation Options icon, then Show Tabs.
- Click on the Collapse a Ribbon button in the bottom-right part of the ribbon.
- Hold down Ctrl+F1.

To temporarily redisplay the ribbon

1. Select any tab title to open it until you select a command or exit the ribbon.

To permanently redisplay the ribbon

Do any of the following:
- Double-click any tab title.
- In the program window's upper-right corner, select the Ribbon Display Options button, then Show Tabs and Commands.
- Press Ctrl+F1.

To optimize the ribbon for touch interaction

1. Click or press a Touch/Mouse Mode button on a Quick Access Toolbar, then Touch.

To specify the items that appear on the status bar

1. To access the Configure Status Bar menu, right-click the status bar. Each item with a check mark is presently enabled.
2. Use the mouse to activate or disable the status bar indication or

tool. The modification takes effect immediately. The menu stays open to allow for numerous choices. When you're finished, click to dismiss the menu.

Chapter 2: Managing Presentations

PowerPoint makes it simple to produce successful presentations for a broad range of audiences. Business leaders no longer use PowerPoint presentations merely to provide information at committee meetings. They are often used to communicate information in corporate and educational contexts, not just in group presentations but as well as in digital communications and online environments. PowerPoint presentations are given as homework tasks to even elementary school pupils. Whether you need to submit a budget to a BOD or persuade leadership to invest in new equipment, PowerPoint can help you get a job done in a competent, visually attractive manner.

PowerPoint's advanced presenting capabilities are simple to identify and use, so even inexperienced users can work efficiently with it with just a short introduction. Many of the procedures you conduct with slide material are similar to those you perform with Microsoft Word docs and Microsoft Excel spreadsheets, so you may be comfortable with them if you are already using another Microsoft Office software. PowerPoint has processes that are particular to the production and administration of presentations.

This chapter walks you through the steps of generating presentations, opening and browsing presentations, showing various presentation views, displaying and altering presentation attributes, and saving and terminating presentations.

2.1 Create Presentations

When making a new presentation, you may start with a blank presentation or one that is built on a template. Unlike Word and Excel templates, most PowerPoint templates manage theme aspects (colors, fonts, and visual effects) and slide designs instead of content templates that give purpose-specific placeholder information. Because each template has an associated theme, you may make a presentation using one template but completely modify its look by using a different theme.

When you launch PowerPoint, you'll get a Start screen with choices for launching a previous presentation or creating a brand-new one.

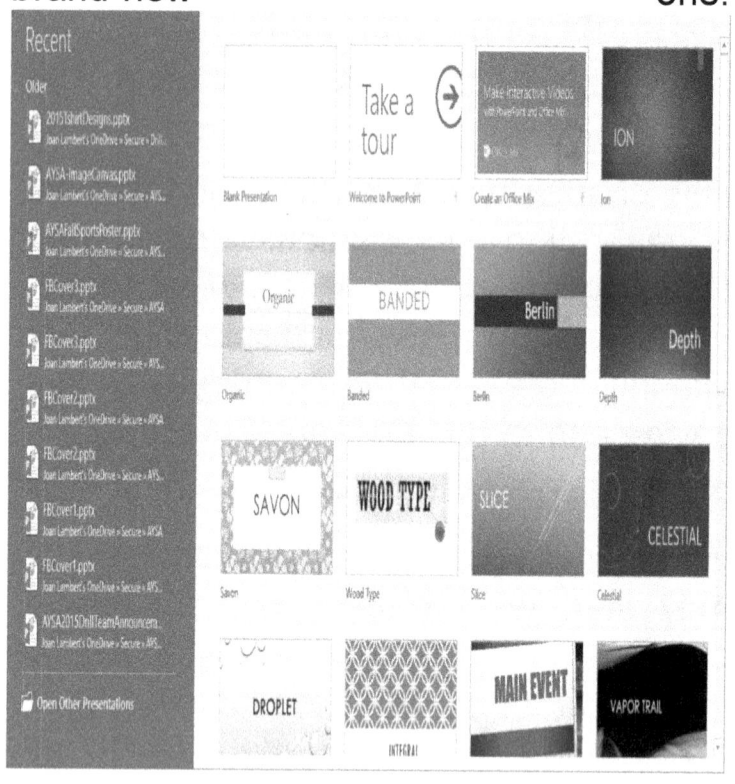

There are many methods to begin a new presentation. When this screen opens, use the Esc key to start a new presentation in PowerPoint. You can also make presentations from the following sources by selecting from the presentation previews and links:

- No presentation If you wish to create and prepare a presentation from the start, you may start with a Blank Presentation design. A fresh, blank presentation has simply a blank headline; it is up to you to add slideshows and slide material, apply a design, and make any custom configuration modifications that are required. Creating appealing, practical presentations from scratch takes effort and needs a good understanding of PowerPoint.

While reading this book, you will get the necessary abilities.

- Template for design You may save time by modeling your presentations on one of PowerPoint's numerous design templates. A layout design is an empty presentation with a pre-applied theme. It may feature backdrop visual elements and customized slide layouts at times. Some templates include simply title slides and leave it up to you to create the other slides; other templates

provide an instance of each of the potential slide layouts.
- Content design template Many prepopulated PowerPoint templates are available for viewing and download from an Office website. These templates provide not only aesthetic components but also contain ideas for various sorts of presentations, such as surveys or product launches. You just change the material supplied in the template to match your requirements after downloading it.

When creating a presentation with PowerPoint, you should be aware that you have two slide-dimensional options, which are known (somewhat erroneously) as slide sizes. Widescreen (16:9) is the default slide size, which is suited for displays like those seen on many computer monitors and desktop screens these days.

Standard slides fit tablet screens

The dimensions of the slide aren't as significant as the aspect ratio. The slides in presentations created using the Blank

Presentation template are configured to Widescreen size by default.

The default sliding size of each template is shown when you show the built-in designs on a New page of a Backstage view. The majority of the templates are 16:9; however, you can simply filter the templates to see just those that are specially made for 4:3 slides.

Before you begin adding information to a new presentation, evaluate how the demonstration will be seen and choose the best slide size. It is best to choose the slide size before the presentation template. You may adjust the slide size after you've created the slide deck, but doing so may cause visual components (particularly those on master slides) to seem different, as well as text and other slide components to not fit on PowerPoint as intended.

Whether you build a blank presentation or one based on a layout template, the presentation lives only in the memory of your computer until you save it.

To create a new blank presentation

1. Launch PowerPoint.
2. Press the Esc key whenever the Start screen displays.

Or

1. If PowerPoint is currently open, choose the File tab to see the Backstage view.
2. In the Backstage view's left pane, click New to open the New page.
3. On the Backstage view's New tab, select the Blank Presentation icon.

To preview presentation design templates

1. Open the Backstage view, then click New in the left pane.
2. Scroll the pane on the New page to see the presentation-style templates that have been installed with PowerPoint.
3. Click any picture to see a preview window with the chosen design's title slide and other color schemes and graphic backdrops.

Do any of the following:

• Use the More Pictures arrows to see more slide layouts for a template.

• Click one of the images in the preview window's right side to apply that color scheme to a slide design of the chosen template.

• To examine alternative design templates, use the arrows to the right or left of the preview window.

• Click the Create button to make a presentation using the active template in a preview window.

• Click the Dismiss button in the upper-right side of a preview window to close a preview session without generating a presentation.

To display only presentation templates that are optimized at the 4:3

slide size

1. On the Backstage view's New tab, underneath the Search field, click 4:3.

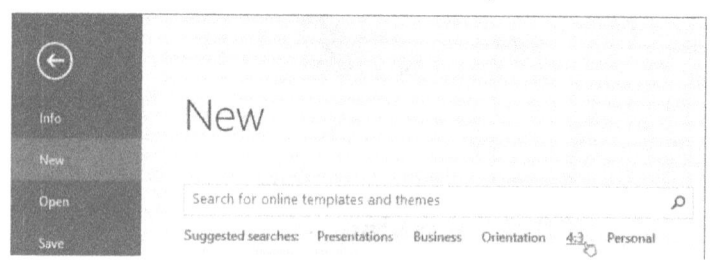

To create a presentation based on a default design template

1. Open the Backstage view's New page.
2. Scroll through the window until you find the design you wish to use.

Carry out one of the following actions:

- To make the presentation, double-click the thumbnail.
- To make the presentation, click the Create icon in a preview box after previewing the design template with the thumbnail.

The new presentation is shown in PowerPoint's Normal view. The title slider is accessible in both the Thumbnails and Slide panes.

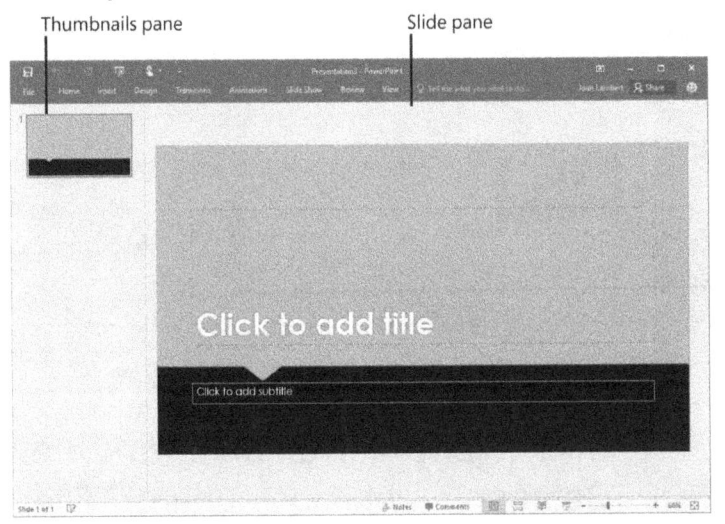

Thumbnails pane   Slide pane

To create a presentation based on an online template

1. Open the Backstage view's New page.
2. Enter a phrase relating to the filler content or design you're searching for in a search box at the page's top, and then select the Search button.

Alternatively, pick one of the recommended searches below the search field.

1. Click any category in the Category list to further filter a template.
2. Scroll through the window to choose a design that meets your requirements.
3. Click any image to sample the graphic, and then click a More Images button to examine the template's content. Then, in the preview box, click the Create button to start creating the presentation.

Or

To make a presentation based on a template, double-click any thumbnail.

To disable the display of the Start screen

1. Click Options in the Backstage view to access the PowerPoint Options dialogue box.
2. Clear the Show on the Start screen whenever this program begins; check the box on the General tab of the dialogue box.

The PowerPoint Options dialogue box should now be closed.

2.2 Display Different Views of Presentations

The aspects of a display that you want to see alter based on what you're doing with a presentation at the time. You may vary the size of the material in the app window, switch between conventional presentation views, and customize the components visible in each view.

Display standard views

PowerPoint offers six perspectives for creating, organizing, and previewing presentations. The following are the opinions:

- **Standard view** This view comprises the Thumbnails pane on the app window's left side, the Slide window on the right side, and an optional Notes window at the bottom. In a Thumbnails pane, you insert, copy, cut, paste, remove the slide, and duplicate; in the Slide pane, you generate slide content; and in the Comments pane, you record slide notes.
- **Page View Notes** This is the only view that allows you to make speaker notes with components other than text. Although you may put speaker notes in a Notes tab in Normal mode, adding images, tables, graphs, or charts to the notes requires you to be in Notes Page view.
- **Overview** This view shows the presentation's text outline in an Outline pane and the current slide in the Slide window. Text may be entered directly on the presentation or in an outline.
- **Reading perspective** Each slide covers the screen in this configuration, which is perfect for previewing the

presentation. To navigate through or go to certain slides, use the navigation bar buttons.

- **Slide Show mode** The presentation is shown as a full-screen photo gallery, commencing with a current slide. It merely shows the slides, not the presenter's features.
- **View of Slide Sorter** This view shows thumbnails for each slide in the presentation. You handle the slides rather than the presentation content in this view. You may quickly rearrange the slides, divide them into parts, and add transitions to one or more slides. You may also use transitions to go from one slide to the next and decide how long every slide should stay on the screen.

When creating presentations, you'll most likely utilize the Normal view and the Slide Sorter view.

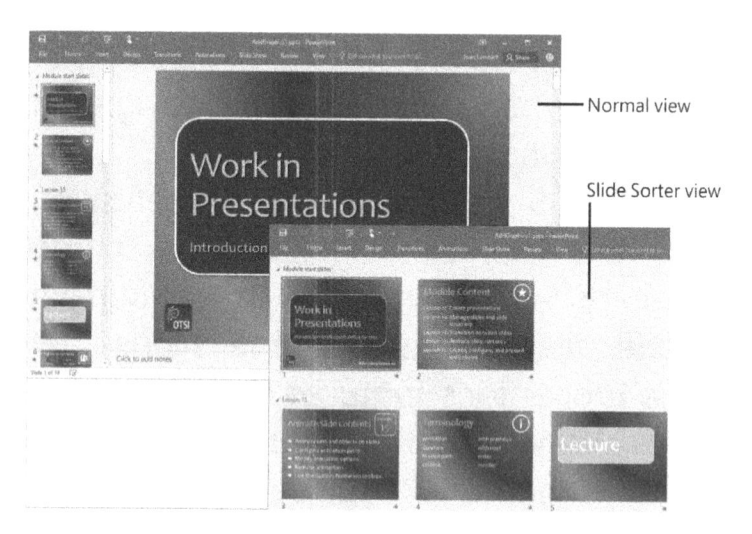

The Display Shortcuts toolbar on the right end of a status bar and the View tab of a ribbon provides access to view choices.

Displaying a presentation in Slide Show mode allows you to evaluate it (or give it to an audience). Each slide covers the screen in this mode, and PowerPoint applies animations, transitions and media effects as you choose. You have the option of starting the PowerPoint presentation from the first slide or the actual operating slide.

To switch among development views of a presentation

Choose one of the following options:

- On the Display Shortcuts toolbar, choose Normal or Slide Sorter.
- In a Presentation Views group on the View tab, select a Normal or Slide Sorter option.

To display a presentation in Slide Show view from the first slide

Choose one of the following options:

- In a Start Slide Showing group on a Slide Show tab, click on From Beginning button. (The ScreenTip that shows when you click on this button states Start From Beginning.)
- Press F5.

To display a presentation in Slide Show view from the current slide

Try any of the following:

- Select the Slide Show option from the View Shortcuts toolbar.
- In a Start Slide Show group on a Slide Show tab, click the
- The button From the Current Slide. (When you place your finger at this

button, the
- The screen tip that shows states, "Begin from This Slide.")
- Press Shift+F5.

To navigate a presentation in Slide Show view

Do this:

- To bring up the Slide Show menu, just move the mouse. To go forward or backward, use the next or previous buttons on the toolbar.

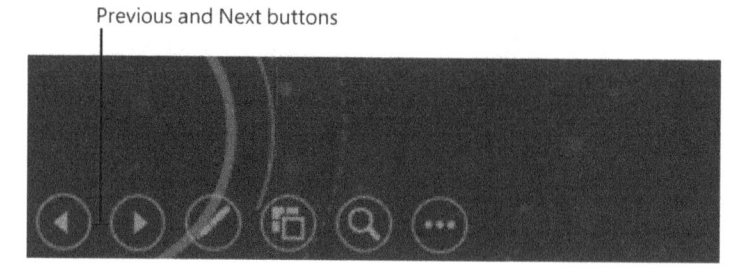

Previous and Next buttons

- To get to the next slide, use the N (next), Enter, Down Arrow, Right Arrow, or Page Down keys.
- If you want to go back a slide, use the P key (for previous), Backspace, the left arrow key, the up-arrow key, or the Page Up key.
- To see the first slide, use the "Home" button.

- To see the last slide, use the End key.
- To exit back to the regular or slide sorter view, use the ESC key.

To display a presentation in the Reading view

Do one of the two options below:
- To switch to Reading View, choose it from the View Shortcuts toolbar.
- To switch to reading mode, go to the View tab and choose Reading View from the Presentation Views submenu.

To navigate a presentation in the Reading view

Take any action from the list below:
- To advance the slide show by one, use N (for next), Enter, the right arrow key, the down arrow key, or the page down key.
- To go back to one slide, use the P key (for the previous), Backspace, the left arrow key, the up arrow key, or the Page Up key.
- To see the first slide, press the Home button.

- To see the last slide, use the End key.
- Revert to Normal or Sliding Sorter view by pressing Esc or selecting the appropriate button from the View Shortcuts toolbar.

Display program elements

You may modify the available real estate for an app window component by resizing the panes or hiding the ribbon.

To adjust the size of the Thumbnails pane in the Normal view

Follow one of these two options:

1. To enlarge or conceal the Thumbnails window, point to its right edge and drag in either direction.
2. If the Thumbnails window has been buried, you may bring it back up by clicking the Thumbnails icon at the very top of the bar.
3. Notes pane visibility in Normal view
4. To access your notes, choose the Notes icon from the status bar.

To adjust the size of the Notes pane in the Normal view

1. In order to enlarge or conceal the Notes pane, point to the boundary between the notes pane and the Slide pane, and when the cursor transforms to a bar with opposed arrows, drag it up or down.

To hide the ribbon in Normal, Outline, or Slide Sorter views

Do any of the following:

- To hide the ribbon, press Ctrl+F1 or click the button that looks like an up-pointing arrow at the right side of the ribbon.
- When the ribbon is collapsed, the tab names remain visible, but the groups and icons are hidden.

To temporarily redisplay the Ribbon

- Select a tab name.
- The ribbon is visible until you press a button on it or move your mouse away from it.

To permanently redisplay the Ribbon

Do any of the following:
- Double-click any tab title.
- Click any tab name, then the Pin a ribbon button, which looks like a pushpin.
- Hold down Ctrl+F1.

Change the display of content

You may quickly switch between open presentations. You may ease the process of comparing or working with the material of many presentations by presenting them side by side.

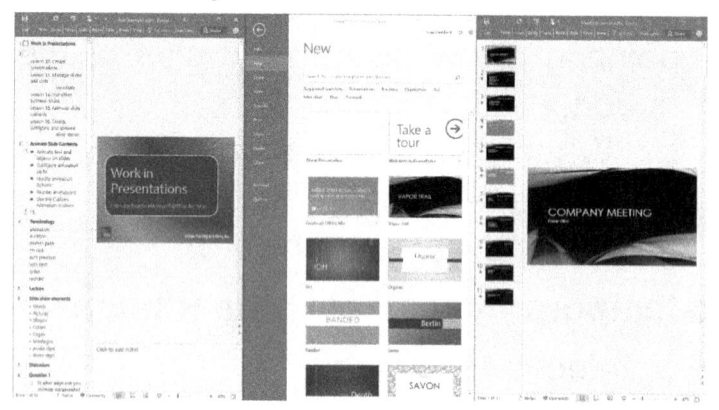

You may show gridlines, rulers and guides in the Slide window and modify the magnification of a current slide to help you place and align slide items more accurately.

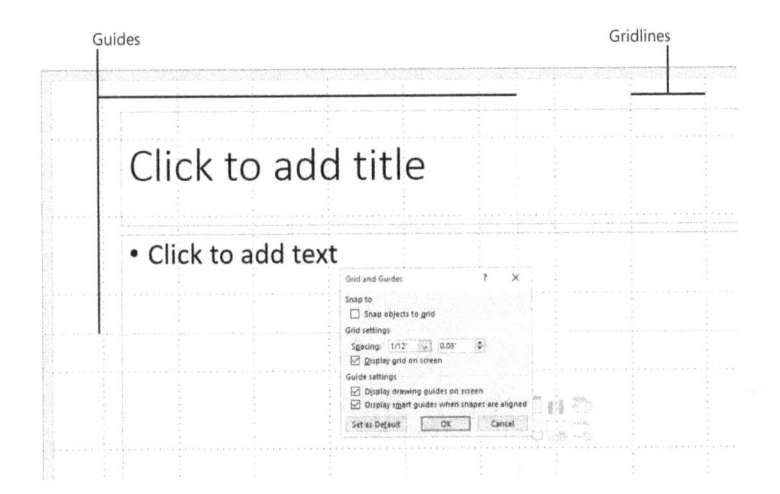

Gridlines are dotted lines that indicate precise units of measurement on a slide. Gridlines may be adjusted within Grid and Guides dialogue box, but they cannot be moved on the slide. Guides are a collection of vertical and horizontal aligning tools that you may move across the Slide pane.

To display a different open presentation

Choose one of the following options:

- In the Window group, on the See tab, click a Switch Windows button, and then select a presentation to view.
- On a Windows taskbar, point to a PowerPoint button, then select the

thumbnail of a presentation you wish to view.

To display multiple open presentations at the same time

1. Click on Arrange All button inside the Window group on the View tab.

To display or hide the ruler, gridlines, and guides

First, toggle the Ruler, Gridlines, and Guides on or off through the View tab's Show group.

To modify the spacing of gridlines

To bring up the Grids and Guides dialogue box, follow these steps:

1. Navigate to the View menu and select the Show dialogue box launcher.
2. To do this, go to the Grid settings section and adjust the Spacing option, which may be done in either fractional or unit measurements. Once you're ready, choose the OK button.

To change the magnification of content in the app window

1. Click a Zoom button to see the Zoom dialogue box on the View tab's Zoom group.

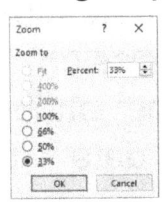

2. In the Zoom dialogue box, click OK after selecting Zoom to choose or enter a percentage in a Percent field.

Or

Perform any of the following in the zoom settings at the correct side of the status bar:
- To lower the zoom percentage, click the Zoom Out button on the left side of the slider.
- To raise the zoom percentage, click on the Zoom In button on the correct side of the slider.
- Click on the Fit slide to present the window button on the correct side of

the status bar.

2.3 Display & Edit Presentation Properties

File characteristics or settings such as the file size, name, date, creation, author, and read-only permission are examples of properties. Some attributes exist in order to offer data to computer applications and operating systems. Properties may be shown inside a presentation (for instance, you can show a slide number on the slide). Some parameters are tracked automatically by PowerPoint, while others are controlled by you.

The Backstage view's Info page allows you to analyze the properties associated with a presentation.

Properties ▾	
Size	764KB
Slides	11
Hidden slides	2
Words	164
Notes	1
Title	Company Meeting
Tags	Add a tag
Comments	Add comments
Multimedia clips	0
Presentation format	Widescreen
Template	Vapor Trail
Status	Add text
Categories	Add a category
Subject	Specify the subject
Hyperlink Base	Add text
Company	Online Training Solutio...
Related Dates	
Last Modified	Today, 10:37 PM
Created	Today, 10:35 PM
Last Printed	Today, 10:37 PM
Related People	
Manager	Specify the manager

Basic properties in a default Properties pane may be changed or removed, or the Properties pane can be expanded to make it more accessible, or the Properties dialogue box can be shown to access far more properties.

To display presentation properties

1. Open the Backstage view's Info page. The standard attributes associated with a display are presented in the right pane's Properties box.
2. Click Display All Properties at the downside of the Properties window to enlarge it.

3. To open the Properties dialogue box, select Properties above the Properties window, followed by Advanced Properties.

To edit presentation properties

1. To begin making changes to a property's value, click a value for that item in the Properties pane. (It's important to keep in mind that you can't change every property. When an editable item is selected, a text box appears. If you try to modify an uneditable one and click it, nothing occurs.
2. Secondly, edit or enter the property's value, and finally, hit Enter.

Or

Select one of the following in the Properties window:

- To change a property's value, go to the Summary page, find the property you want to edit, click the checkbox to the right of it, and then edit the value.
- To change a property's value, go to the page's Custom section and use

the Name list to find the property you wish to change.

2.4 Save & Close Presentations

When saving a presentation for the first time, you may either use the Save button in the Quick Access Toolbar or go into the Backstage view and use the Save As command. In either case, you'll be sent to the save as window, where you may choose a new location for the file.

Some forms of digital information must be made accessible to individuals with impairments in many countries. A presentation's final file format(s) should be known before the presentation is created so that it may be made accessible to users of assistive technology. Certain information may only be seen in Normal mode while using PowerPoint but can be seen in other available file formats, such as tagged PDFs. You should check the template's accessibility before building a presentation on it.

A local folder or, if you're connected to the Internet, a Microsoft OneDrive folder is also an acceptable location for storing the presentation. You may make your SharePoint OneDrive or another SharePoint location accessible from the Places pane of a Save As a page, similar to any other folder if your organization uses Microsoft SharePoint.

You may name the file in the Save As dialogue box by clicking Browse at the downside of the left pane.

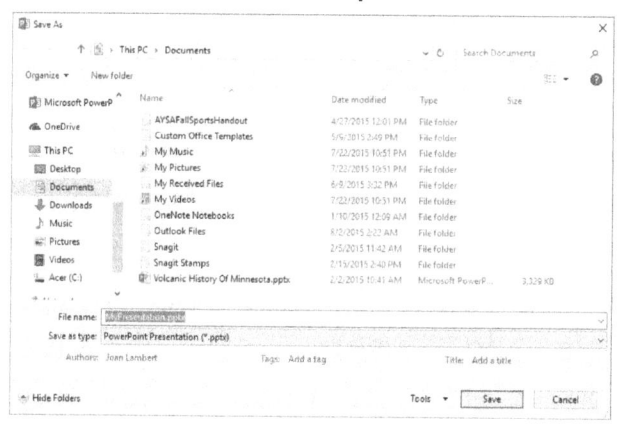

Simply hitting the Save button on the presentation's Quick Access Toolbar will save any further changes. In this way, the updated presentation replaces the prior one.

Show the Save As a page, and save a new version with various names in the same place or in a separate location if you wish to retain both the new and old versions. (Two files that share the same name cannot both exist in the same directory.)

New instances of PowerPoint are launched whenever a presentation is opened. If you have over one presentation open, you may shut the one you want to leave open by clicking the Close icon at the right end of the presentation's title bar. You may end a single presentation while leaving PowerPoint open by going to the Backstage window and then clicking Close.

To save a presentation

1. To access the Save As a page in the Backstage view, use the Save button on the Quick Access Toolbar.
2. Once you've decided where to save the file, click the Browse button in the right pane to bring up the Save As dialogue box.
3. To get to the location of your files, just use the usual Windows

methods.
4. You may save your presentation to your computer by following these steps: 4. Give your presentation a name in the File name box, and then click Save.

Or

1. Save a previous presentation with the same name and location by pressing Ctrl+S.

To close a presentation

Try any of the following:

- To exit the presentation and the app window, choose Close from the title bar's right end.
- To end the presentation without quitting the program, you may bring up the Backstage view by clicking Close.
- You may end a presentation by pointing to its thumbnail on the Windows Taskbar, selecting it, and then clicking the Close button, which appears in the presentation's upper-right corner.

Save files to OneDrive

You can use OneDrive to save documents, whether you're in the office or at home. Your company's SharePoint site or a personal cloud storage space tied to your Microsoft account is both possible destinations for your saved files when using OneDrive. When you save a file in any kind of OneDrive storage, you have the choice of sharing it with others.

You can save a presentation to your OneDrive by going to the Save As tab in the presentation's backstage area, selecting your OneDrive, and afterward choosing the destination you'd want to save it to.

The destination folder in OneDrive is where you'd want to save the file. When your

In the event that your desired OneDrive doesn't display in the list of places, choose to Add A Place, then select OneDrive, and then provide the related credentials.

When you upload a Presentation slide to OneDrive, you and anyone else who has access to it may make changes to it in either your locally installed copy of

PowerPoint or in the web-based PowerPoint Online.

Microsoft account customers may make use of 1 TB of free cloud storage space on OneDrive. Access your OneDrive from any Office app or at onedrive.live.com if you have a Microsoft account. Sign up for a free Microsoft account at signup.live.com, or use any existing email address to get started. (You may also create a new email account there if you don't already have one that you wish to use for this.)

Storage in OneDrive for Business is handled centrally by your business or SharePoint service provider if you're using it as part of a SharePoint 2023 setup.

Chapter 3: Manage & Create Slides

When you start a presentation using a design template, the only slide that appears is the title slide. It is up to you to add extra slides for the material that you want to include in the presentation. You may either construct slides based on slide templates meant to carry various sorts of material or copy existing slides from previous presentations.

When creating a presentation with several slides, you may divide them into parts. Sections are not clearly visible, but they make working with slide material in logical pieces simpler. A logical presentation and also an overall consistent design, punctuated by changes that add weight precisely where it is required, may increase the possibility that the message you want to express is received by your target audience.

This chapter walks you through the steps of adding and deleting slides, segmenting presentations, rearranging slides, applying theme sections, and altering slide backgrounds.

3.1 Add & Remove Slides

The slide layouts connected with the slide master that is part of the design template determine the look and structure of the slides.

- Slide backdrops and included graphics are examples of slide layouts.
- Text box sizes, forms, and locations
- Each text box location's default paragraphs and character formats.
- Regular headers and footers.

A slide master could just have one slide layout but usually feature distinct slide layouts for slides displaying the presentation title, section names, and various combinations of slide names and content, as well as a blank slide with merely the backdrop. Each slide arrangement is titled; the name implies the principal use of the slide layout, but you are not restricted to that recommendation; you may insert any sort of material and adjust the layout of any slide. The New Slide menu displays the possible slide layouts in a presentation.

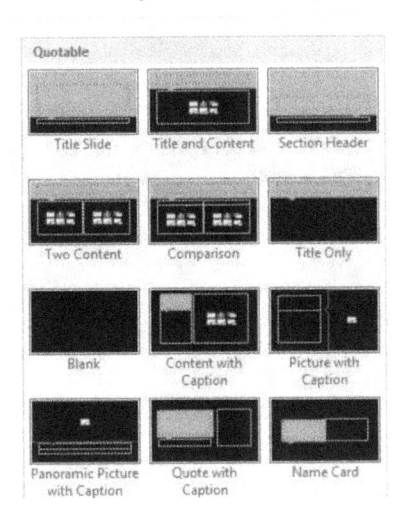

You can change the built-in slide layouts, make your own, or construct completely new sets of slide layouts known as slide masters, and you may reset slides to fit their slide layouts or apply various slide layouts to existing slides.

3.2 Insert New Slides

PowerPoint places a new slide after the presently active slide when you create one. When creating a new presentation using a normal PowerPoint template, any slides added after the title slide will use the Title And Content layout, and any slides added after any other slide will use the layout of the slide they follow.

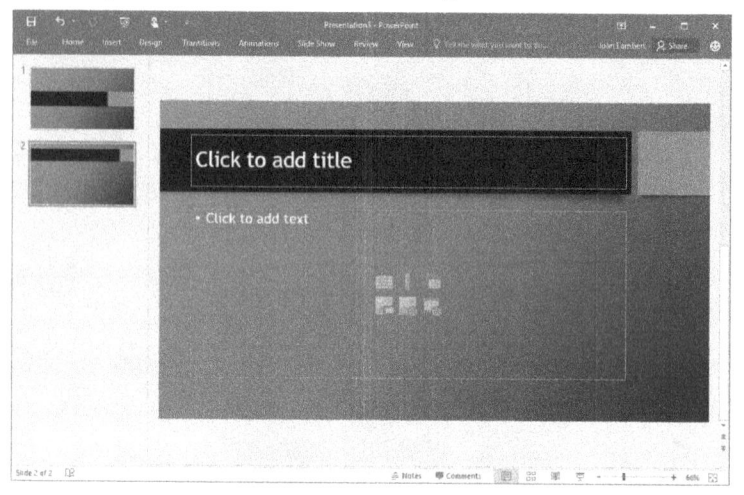

If you wish to add a slide with a different layout, you may either pick the layout while inserting the slide or alter the slide layout after creating the slide.

To add a slide based on the default slide layout

1. Choose the slide to which you would like to add the new one.

Choose one of the following options:

- In the Slides group on the Home tab, select the New Slide button (not its arrow).
- Hold down Ctrl+M.

To add a slide based on any slide layout

1. Choose the slide to which you would like to add a new one.
2. On the Home tab, inside the Slides group, select the New Slide arrow to open the gallery and menu for New Slide.
3. Inside the gallery, click a thumbnail of a slide arrangement to add a slide based on that slide layout.

Copy and import slides and content

You can reuse presentations from one briefing in another in one of two ways: copy the slides from the primary research given to the new presentation or use the Reuse Slides tool, which exhibits the material of an original presentation and enables you to select which slides to insert in a new presentation.

You may copy an existing slide inside a presentation to use it as the foundation for a new slide. Instead of starting from scratch, you may then tweak the cloned slide.

You don't have to recreate a slide that welcomes you to the audience if you use it regularly in your presentations. You may simply use a slide from one presentation in another. (You may use the same approaches to reuse a slide from another person's presentation in order to standardize the look or structure of slide content with other people in your company.) Unless you specify differently, the slide inherits the style of its new presentation.

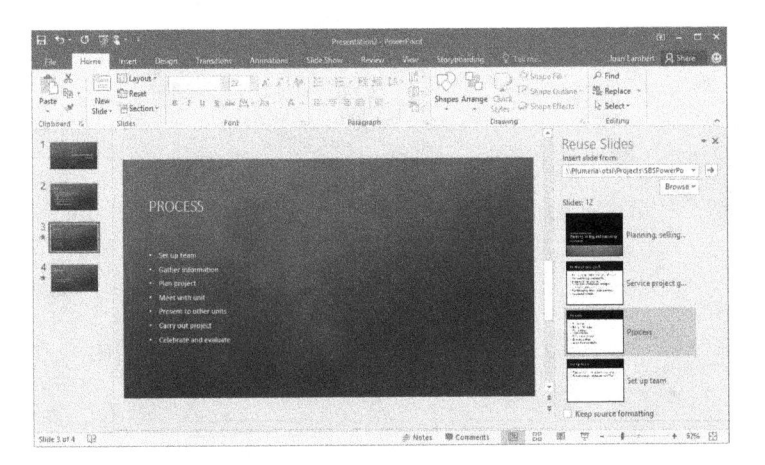

If the material of your presentation is already in a document, you may arrange it in format, e.g., and then import it into PowerPoint. Format the document information that you wish to integrate into a presentation as headers to ensure a seamless import procedure. Some styles are converted into slide headers by PowerPoint, while others are converted into bullet points.

Heading 1

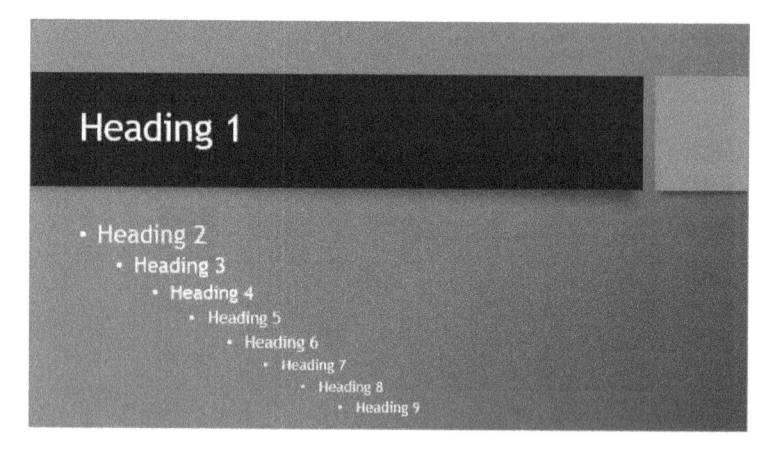

- Heading 2
  - Heading 3
    - Heading 4
      - Heading 5
        - Heading 6
          - Heading 7
            - Heading 8
              - Heading 9

The table below shows how PowerPoint transforms Word document styles into PowerPoint presentation components.

Word document style	PowerPoint presentation style
Title, Subtitle, Heading 1, any bulleted list level, or any numbered list level	Slide title
Heading 2	First-level bulleted list item
Heading 3	Second-level bulleted list item
Heading 4	Third-level bulleted list item
Heading 5	Fourth-level bulleted list item
Heading 6	Fifth-level bulleted list item
Heading 7	Sixth-level bulleted list item
Heading 8	Seventh-level bulleted list item
Heading 9	Eighth-level bulleted list item

Select a single slide

Do any of the following:

Do some of the following:

- In the Thumbnails window, click any slide in Normal mode.

- In the Outline view, click the Outline pane's slide header.
- In the Slide Sorting system view, choose a slide from the Slide window.

To select multiple slides

1. In Normal, Outline, or Slide Sorter views, click the first slide to pick.

Choose one of the following options:

- To choose a succession of slides in a row, hold down the Shift key and then click the final slide you wish to select.
- To pick noncontiguous slides, hold down the Ctrl key while clicking each subsequent slide.

To insert a copy of a slide immediately following the original slide

1. View the presentation in Normal mode.
2. In the Thumbnails window, right-click the slide you wish to duplicate and choose Duplicate Slide.

To insert a copy of one or more slides anywhere in a presentation

1. Open the presentation in Normal or Slide Sorter mode.

To replicate a slide or slides, do one of the following:

- Select the slide thumbnail or pictures, then press Ctrl+C or select the Copy button in the Clipboard group on the Home tab.
- Right-click a slideshow thumbnail and choose Copy.

To add the slide copy or copies, do one of the following:

- Either select the thumbnail into which you wish to put the slide copy or click the empty space following the thumbnail. Then, on the Home tab, under the Clipboard group, hit Ctrl+V or select the Paste button.
- Right-click where you wish to insert a slide copy or copies, and then pick the Use Destination Theme or Keep Source Formatting option in the Paste Options area of the shortcut menu.

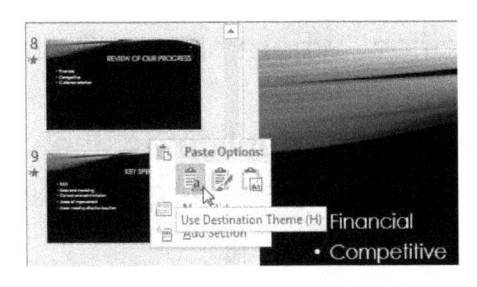

Step 3 should be repeated to insert extra copies of the presentation or slides into the presentation.

To insert a slide from another presentation

1. Launch PowerPoint and open the source and destination presentations. Display each presentation in either Normal or Slide Sorter mode.
2. Show both PowerPoint tabs side by side.
3. Select the slide or slides to copy from the source presentation.
4. Move the selection to the target presentation by dragging it. In Normal mode, a horizontal line between slide thumbnails or a vertical line between thumbnails in the Slide Sorting system view

specifies where PowerPoint will put the slides.
5. PowerPoint duplicates the slides and applies the target theme to the duplicates.

Or

1. Open the destination presentations in Standard mode.
2. In the Slides group, on the Home or Insert tab, click a New Slide arrow.
3. Click Reuse Slides on the New Slide menu underneath the gallery to open the Reuse Slides window on the right-hand side of the screen.

Click on the Browse button, followed by Browse File. Browse to a folder containing the presentation from which you wish to utilize slides in the Browse dialogue box, then double-click your presentation.

3.3 Divide Presentations Into Sections

You may break a larger presentation into parts to make it simpler to organize and structure. Sections are identified by titles over their slides in both Normal and Slide Sorter views. They do not display in other views, nor do they produce slides or otherwise disrupt the presentation's flow.

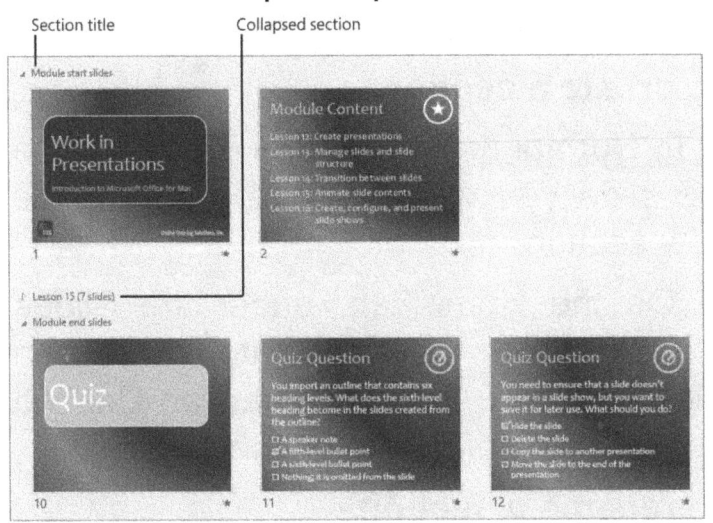

Sections make it easy to concentrate on one aspect of a slideshow at a time since you may collapse whole sections to show simply the section headings.

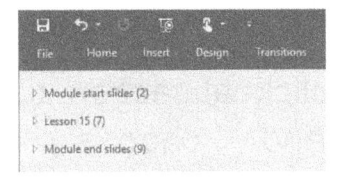

Some designs provide a slide layout for section separator slides that is comparable to the title slide style. If you split a lengthy presentation into topic-based portions, you may wish to move your section titles to all of these slides to give audience assistance or to indicate logical areas in a presentation to take pauses or answer questions.

To create a section

1. In Normal or Slide Sorter view, choose the slide you want to be the first in the new section.

2. On the Home tab, under the Slides group, click a Section button and then click on Add Section to enter an Untitled Section title before the chosen slide.

To rename a section

> 1. To open a Rename Section dialogue box in Normal or Slide Sorter view, perform one of the following:

- Right-click a section title to be changed and choose Rename Section.
- Click the Section button in the Slides group on the Home tab, then click Rename Section.

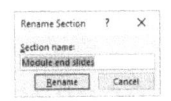

> 1. Replace or update the current section name in a Section name field, then click a Rename button.

To collapse or expand one slide section

1. In Normal or Slide Sorter mode, click the arrow next to the section title.

To collapse or expand all slide sections

Choose one of the following options:
- In the Slides group on the Home tab, select the Section button, then Collapse All or Extend All.
- Right-click a section name and choose to Expand All or Collapse All from the menu.

3.4 Rearrange Slides & Sections

When creating a presentation, it's common to add many slides and then rearrange them for optimal flow and impact.

Slides and slide groups may be moved around in a presentation to create new layouts.

When presenting, for change slides

For reordering slideshow thumbnails, start by selecting them in Normal or Slide Sorter view. As you drag, you'll see the other thumbnails reposition to show you where the chosen slide will appear after you let go of the mouse button.

Or

First, choose the thumbnail of the slide you want to cut, and then either press Ctrl+X or go to the Home tab and pick Cut in the Clipboard group.

Choose one of the two options below:

- Select the thumbnail of the slide you wish to place the clipped slide on afterward, and then either press Ctrl+V or select Paste from the Clipboard menu.

To relocate a slide, you must first:

- Click between two or more of the slide thumbnails to place a thin red marking (horizontal in the Preview pane or vertical in the Slide Sorter view). When you're ready to paste, either use Ctrl+V or go to Edit > Paste in the Clipboard submenu.

Or

1. Right-click the thumbnail of the slide, and choose Cut.
2. Right-click the area in between the other image thumbnails to which you wish to relocate the slide, and then drag it there.
3. Select Use Destination Theme or Keep Source Formatting from the Paste Options submenu of the shortcut menu.

How to Rearrange Sections in a Presentation

1. To select all slides in a certain part for relocation, click the section's title.
2. Move the tab where you want it to go by dragging it.

Or

To move a section and all of its slides to a new location, right-click a section title and choose Move Section Above or Move Section Down, respectively.

The process of eliminating the boundary between two sections in order to integrate them into one

To separate a set of slides, follow these steps:

1. Click the title of the subset you want to separate.
2. You may delete a section by clicking the Section button under the Slides group on the Home page and then selecting Remove Section.

Or

To delete a section, just right-click its heading and choose the option.

To combine all sections by removing section titles

1. First, choose the Section button (located inside the Slides group on the Home page) and then click Erase All Sections.

How to remove certain slides from a presentation?

1. In order to erase an entire group of slides, you must first select all of those slides by clicking the title of that group.
2. Simply hit the Delete key twice.

Or

1. To delete a section, right-click its heading, and choose the option to Delete Section and Slides.

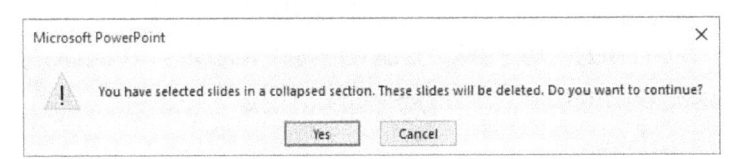

Microsoft PowerPoint
You have selected slides in a collapsed section. These slides will be deleted. Do you want to continue?
Yes   Cancel

2. First, choose the title of the section you want to remove together with all of its slides, and then, if PowerPoint asks you to verify the deletion, select Yes.

3.5 Change Slide Backgrounds

A generic backdrop is included with the presentation theme. The backdrop might be a solid color or a graphical element.

You may change the look of your slides by replacing the default backdrop image with a new one in any color, gradient, texture, pattern, or photo. In a Format Background window, you may make these modifications.

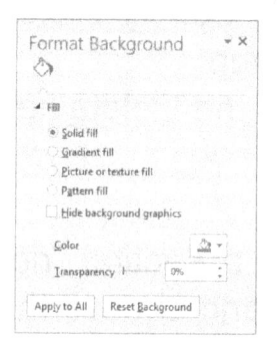

When you click on a particular option in a Format Background window, further customization possibilities become available.

While a backdrop of one solid color is preferable for reading, a color gradient may be used to provide visual interest without overwhelming the eye. PowerPoint has a number of gradient patterns that transition from bright to dark and dark to light, depending on the color scheme.

Also, you may make your own two-color, three-color, or color gradients. A gradient's color transitions are managed by individual "gradient stops." You may choose the starting point and ending color for each gradient stop. Two to ten gradient stops are possible in a color gradient.

Up to 10 different colors may be used in a gradient. The slide backdrop may be given a pattern or design if you'd want something fancy than a plain color or color gradient. There are a number of built-in textures available for use as slide backgrounds in PowerPoint.

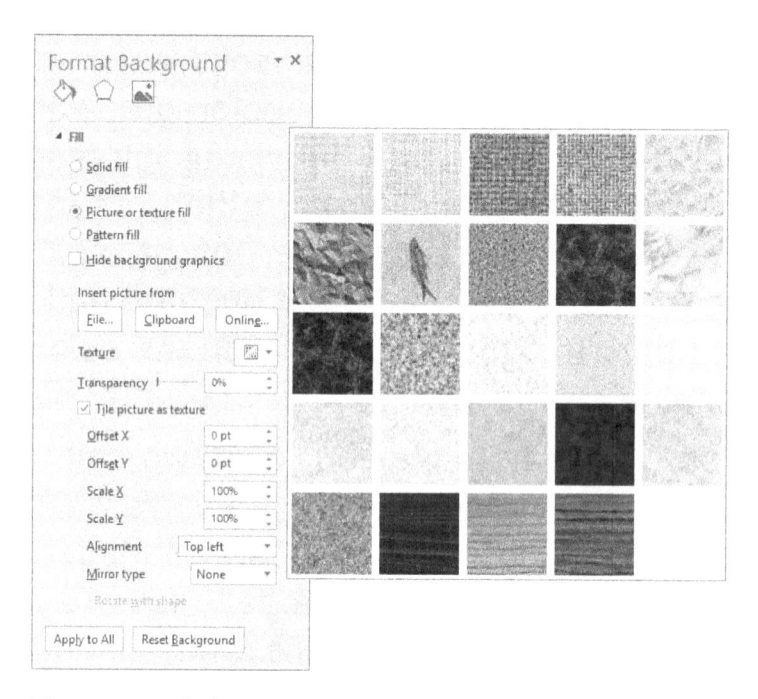

If none of those options work for you, you may try using a photo of a rough surface instead. Include a personal photo for added drama, but remember to limit it to focal points and not the whole slide.

You may choose from one of 48 different patterns and customize a background and foreground colors if you'd rather use a pattern than a texture.

To open the Format Background panel

To change the background, first, go to the Design tab and select a Format

Background button under the Customize subheading.

To close a Format Background pane

To take action, you can:
- To dismiss the window, click the X in its upper-right corner (the X).
- Just click the arrow to the right of the pane's name and then select Close.
- So that a new backdrop is used for every slide
- To begin customizing the slide background, go to the Format > Background menu.
- Select the Apply to Every button located at the lower side of the window.

Getting rid of a theme's custom background image from a slide

1. Open the Format Background window.
2. Choose the "Hide background graphics" option in a Format Background window.

How to give one or more slides a solid background color?

1. To begin, choose Solid fill in a Format Background submenu.
2. Secondly, open the color picker by clicking the Color button.

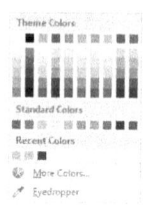

1. Select a color from the theme's color palette, a solid color, a recently used color, or More Colors to create your own.
2. The transparency of the background color may be changed by dragging the Transparency slider or entering a percentage value.

To apply a gradient background color to one or more slides

1. First, choose Gradient and fill in a Format Background section.

2. To use one of the predefined gradients, just choose one by clicking the Preset gradients icon and picking a color from the palette that appears.

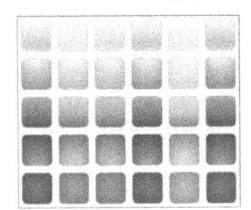

Or

1. 1 Select a type from the drop-down menu, such as Linear, Rectangular, Radial, Path, or Shadow from Title.
2. Click the drop-down arrow next to Direction, then choose the desired gradient direction.
3. If you choose Linear as your type, you may set the gradient's inclination. If you know the angle, type it into the Angle box.

Enter the desired gradient stops in a Gradient Stops section by either:

- To move the marker on the slider, use an Add color stop option.

- To add a gradient stop, move the slider to a position about where you want it.

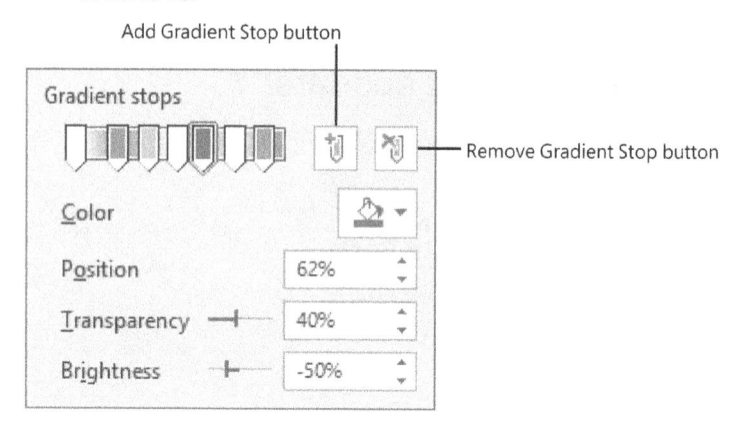

```
Add Gradient Stop button

Gradient stops
                          Remove Gradient Stop button
Color
Position      62%
Transparency  40%
Brightness    -50%
```

You can get rid of gradient stops by doing one of two things in a Gradient Stops section:

- To get rid of a gradient stop, drag the slider to where the marker is. If you want to undo the gradient's stop, select it and then click the corresponding button.
- Pull the gradient endpoint indicator out of the way of the slider.

Customize the gradient's colors, locations, opacities, and brightness in the box labeled "Gradient stops." Bear in mind the following:

- The eyedropper tool allows you to choose a color from a palette or to precisely duplicate an existing hue.

Adjust the opacity and brightness by dragging the markers on a slider, typing in new values in the percentage fields, or turning the dials.

To apply a textured background to one or more slides

1. First, choose a Picture or pattern and fill in a Format Background section.
2. You may access the texture library by clicking the Texture icon. You may choose from many different textured backgrounds, such as marble, wood grain, granite, and Formica-like patterns in a wide range of colors.
3. Third, choose a texture from the gallery and click it to use it.
4. Adjust the background color's opacity by dragging the Transparency slider or entering a percentage value.

Chapter 4: Manage & Insert Text On Slides

In later chapters, you'll learn how to add special effects to your electronic presentations and wow your audience. But if the text on the slides isn't up to snuff, no amount of animation, jazzy colors, and accompanying graphics will help.

PowerPoint presentations are an alternate distribution style for reports because of the ease with which information may be presented creatively using the floating components that are a hallmark of a PowerPoint slide.

Text will serve as the basis for the vast majority of your presentations. Titles and other text on slides should still perform their job, and they should do it effectively, even if you follow the current trend of creating presentations that consist mostly of photographs.

Step-by-step instructions are provided in this chapter for inserting text into slides, rearranging and erasing text, formatting characters and paragraphs, adding

WordArt text effects, verifying spelling and selecting the most appropriate phrasing.

4.1 Enter Text On Slides

In PowerPoint presentations, placeholders are used to specify the kind and location of items on each slide. There might be spaces for a title and a bulleted list with points and one or more layers of secondary subpoints, for instance, on a single slide. Slides may have new text added to them, or content may be entered into the already placeholders.

Enter text in placeholders

In Normal mode, you can type into a placeholder on a slide in the Slide pane;

in Outline view, the complete presentation is presented in outline form; and in both views, you may edit the text in the Outline pane.

The pointer transforms into an I-beam if it is above an outline or text placeholder. A flashing cursor appears at the point where you click; here is where your text will go. When you type, your words immediately show on the slide as well as in the outline or slide preview (Normal view) (Outline view).

PowerPoint's AutoFit function automatically adjusts the size of the text to suit the available space. PowerPoint automatically adjusts the text size to suit the placeholder if you insert more text than will fit in it. To the left of a placeholder in PowerPoint, you'll see the AutoFit Options option if PowerPoint needs to resize the text to fit the placeholder. On the AutoFormat As You Type page of the AutoCorrect dialogue box, you have the option of customizing AutoFit for each individual placeholder or for all placeholders at once.

To enter text in a placeholder

Do one of the following things:

- The slide should be seen in Normal mode. To replace the sample text, click on it and type.
- In Outline mode, you may type straight into the slide's accompanying Outline window.

To demote the current text by one level

Do one of the two options below:

To start a new paragraph, hit Tab once the cursor is in the first line.

To do this, first select the Increase List Level button in the Paragraph group on the Home tab.

To promote the current text by one level

Choose one of the two options below:

- Press Shift+Tab to go to the start of the paragraph with the pointer already there.
- To do this, click the Reduce List Level button in a Paragraph group on the Home tab.

You may modify the AutoFit parameters for a specific placeholder by

- First, open the AutoFit Options menu by clicking the AutoFit icon that displays to the left of the placeholder.
- Then, from the option that appears, choose either AutoFit Text to Placeholder or Stop Matching Text to This Placeholder from the AutoFit Options.

Or

In a Format Shape menu, choose Text Options

- Bring up the configuration page for the text box.
- Select either Resize outline to fit the text or Do not Autofit, reduce text on overflow.

If you want to modify the AutoFit parameters for all existing placeholders, then do this:

- The AutoFormat As You Write tab of an AutoCorrect dialogue box may be accessed by clicking the AutoFit button, which will reveal the AutoFit Options menu.

- Select or deselect the choices here on AutoFormat As You Write tab to have the document's title and body content formatted automatically. After that, you should go ahead and click OK.

Insert nonstandard characters

Copyright and trademark symbols, Greek letters, currency symbols, and letters with phonetic symbols are just a few examples of text that can need special characters not found on a conventional keyboard that you may need to use in your presentation slides. You might also supplement the text with directional arrows or visual aids. You may use mathematical operators and other special characters.

PowerPoint's built-in symbol library is extensive, and each one is simple to use. Symbols, much like graphics, may increase a slide's visual information or aesthetic appeal. However, they are not images but rather characters from a particular typeface alphabet, often from the Wingdings family.

The following table lists some often-used key combinations that may be used to insert commonly used symbols. By using AutoCorrect and AutoFormat, you may have the symbols substituted for the key combinations.

Symbol	Description	Key combination
©	Copyright	(c)
®	Registered trademark	(r)
™	Trademark	(tm)
€	Euro	(e)
...	Ellipsis	... (three periods)
—	Em dash	-- (two hyphens followed by a word and space) Or Ctrl+Alt+Minus Sign on numeric keypad
–	En dash	- (space hyphen space followed by a word and space) Or Ctrl+Minus Sign on numeric keypad

1st, 2nd, 3rd, 4th, and so on	Ordinal numbers	1st, 2nd, 3rd, 4th, and so on followed by a space
¼, ½, ¾, and so on	Fractional numbers	1/4, 1/2, 3/4, and so on

Select a typeface that contains symbols, open the Symbol dialogue box, then input the symbol you need from among several hundred options. Using the Symbol dialogue box, you may enter accented characters by choosing them from the list of symbols that correspond to the typeface you're using. Character sets that can be shown in fonts go well beyond basic Latin and Greek.

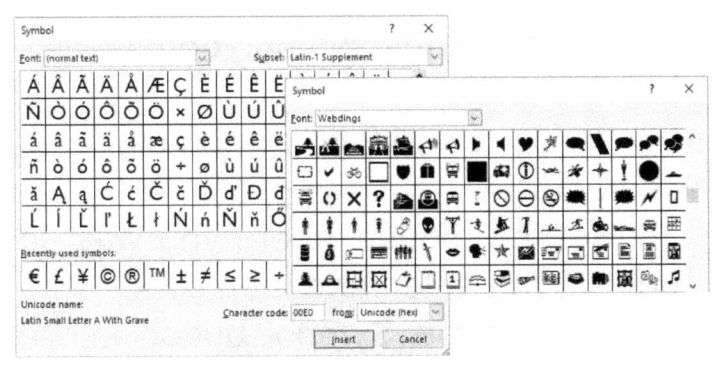

To insert a symbol

First, choose the text anywhere you want to put the symbol.

Select the Symbol button in the Insert tab's Symbols group to bring up the Symbols dialogue box.

Simply open the Font menu in the dialogue box, choose a symbol font (such as Webdings, Symbol or Wingdings), and the corresponding characters will be shown. You may see more characters by scrolling up and down the character window.

To place a sign where the pointer is, you may do one of the following:

- The process of inserting a symbol is as simple as clicking the symbol you require and then clicking the Insert button.
- To activate the symbol, double-click it.
- Incorporating a non-standard character
- Set the mouse where you wish to put the character, and then click.
- Select the Symbol button in the Insert tab's Symbols group.
- Select the typeface you want to use in the Symbol dialogue box by clicking

the Font option and then selecting the font.

Pick the characters you only want to see in the Subset drop-down menu and click Show.

4.2 Move, Copy & Delete Text

If you make a mistake while typing, you may easily fix it using the industry standard methods. Editing single characters are simple, but if you need to make bulk changes, you'll need to learn how to pick text first. Any text you click on will be highlighted on a screen.

Content may be selected using a variety of methods, including the mouse, the keyboard, tapping, and a combination of these. The Mini Toolbar appears in PowerPoint whenever you make a selection, allowing you to rapidly apply a style to the selected material or do additional actions.

Select text on a slide, inside a presentation, or across presentations may be moved or copied using the following methods:

- A selection may be dragged and dropped in a new spot. When both the starting point and the final destination are shown on display at the same time, this way is most convenient.
- If you want to move some text from one place to another, you may do it by cutting or copying it to a Clipboard and then pasting it. Many different techniques exist for modifying text by means of snipping, copying, and pasting. When you clip text in PowerPoint, it disappears from its previous spot regardless of the approach you used. In PowerPoint, the source text is preserved when you copy and paste.

The Clipboard is a shared short-term memory space across Office programs.

The Clipboard window lets you see what has been copied or cut and pasted into the Clipboard.

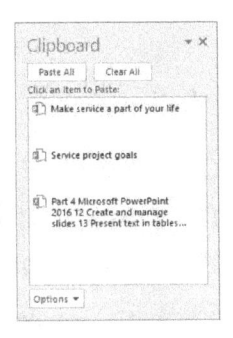

Without bringing up the Clipboard window, you may still cut, copy, and paste content to/from the Clipboard, as well as paste the most recently used item from the Clipboard. By bringing up the Clipboard window, you may access and deal with objects that predate the current selection.

It's simple to undo a recent modification if you make a mistake while editing. You may reverse your most recent action or retry it at a different part of the presentation.

As well as being able to copy and paste text, deleting it is also an option. Using the Delete or Backspace key is the quickest method to do this. If you remove anything by accident using one of these keys, the text isn't copied to the Clipboard, so you can't reuse it.

To select text

Perform any of the following:

- Dragging across the text, selects the words, lines, and paragraphs that are next to the current selection.

Start by putting the cursor at the beginning of the text you wish to choose, and then perform one of the following:

- Hold the Shift key and use the left or right arrow keys to choose a single character.
- Hold down the Shift and Ctrl keys, and then hit the Left Arrow or Right Arrow keys to pick a single word.
- Hold the Shift key and use the up or down arrow to choose a single line at a time.
- While holding the Shift key, click the content's end to select all of the text to the right of it.
- Double-clicking any part of a word will select it. When you use the "find" function in PowerPoint, it will only choose the word and the space following it, but not any punctuation.
- Click the bullet on the slide or in the Outline window to choose the item

from a bulleted list.

Select all the text on a slide by clicking its icon in the Outline panel.

If you click on a slide's empty placeholder and then click the solid border instead of the dashed one, you'll select everything on the slide. Just use the Select menu and then the Select All button to do this.

A paragraph may be selected by using the "triple-click" method on any part of the paragraph.

Pick one word, line, or paragraph; then, while holding down the Ctrl key, select another text segment that is not immediately next to the first.

Either of the following will pick everything in the current blank:

- Select the Select button, and then click Select All on the Home tab's Editing group.
- To select all, use the shortcut Ctrl+A.

To release a selection

1. To deselect a section, click somewhere else in the window.

To cut text to the Clipboard

One can do anything with the text after selecting it:

- The cut may be accessed from the Home tab's Clipboard menu.
- You can cut a selection by right-clicking on it and choosing the appropriate menu option.
- To cut and paste, use Control-X.

To copy text to the Clipboard

You can do anything with the selected text after making the selection:

- To do this, go to the Home tab and then to the Clipboard group.
- Simply copy the selection by right-clicking on it and choosing to copy.
- Ctrl + C to copy.

To insert the most recent Clipboard entry

Enter text, put the cursor where you want it, and then perform one of the following:

- Click the Paste button in the Home tab's Clipboard group.
- To paste, use the Shift + V keys.

Or

- To input text, right-click the spot, choose Paste Options from the context menu, and then select the desired choice.

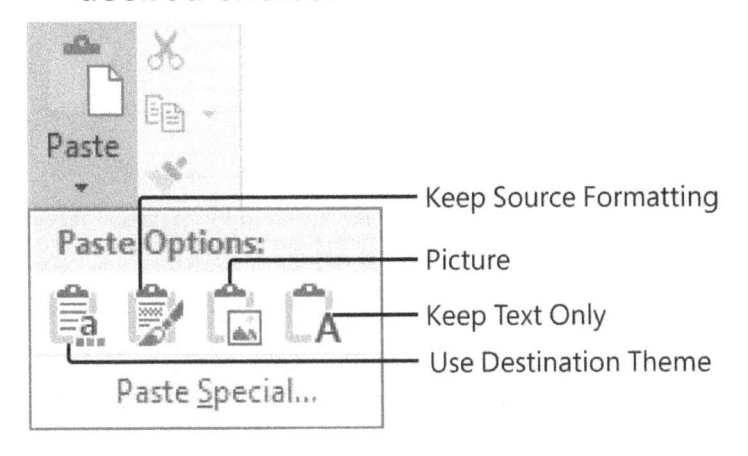

```
Paste
  Paste Options:
       Keep Source Formatting
       Picture
       Keep Text Only
       Use Destination Theme
  Paste Special...
```

To move text

Choose one of the following methods:

- Just grab the text and move it to where you want it to go.

Follow one of these two methods to move text around on your computer:

- Simply highlight the text, right-click, choose "Copy," and then paste it where needed.
- Keep Ctrl pressed and drag a text to where you want it to go.

It's simple to bring up the Clipboard section:

- Find the Clipboard dialogue box on the Home tab and click it to open it.

To manage copied and cut items in a Clipboard pane

To take any action:

- Individual items may be pasted at the cursor by clicking them or by pointing to them and clicking the arrow that appears, followed by Paste.
- Click the Paste All icon at the top of a Clipboard window to paste everything currently copied to the Clipboard into the current window.
- A selection may be deleted from the Clipboard by pointing to it in the Clipboard window, click the arrow that displays, and then selecting Delete.
- Select all of the items in the Clipboard and then hit the Clear All button.

To control the behavior of the Clipboard pane

First, choose the desired viewing mode by clicking Options at the bottom of the window.

To undo your last editing action

Choose one of the two options below:

- First, access the Undo function by clicking the corresponding button in the QAT.
- The key combination to press is Ctrl+Z.

To undo more than one step, do this:

- To undo an activity, first, choose it from the Undo list on a Quick Access Toolbar. The power of the spoken word undoes the previous action and all subsequent ones.

To restore your last editing action

Choose one of the two options below:

- You may undo your last action by selecting it and clicking the redo button on the QAT.
- Select "Ctrl-Y" on your keyboard.
- When you need to get rid of only a few characters
- Put the cursor to a left of a text you wish to get rid of.

- Then, for each unwanted letter, number, or symbol, press the Delete key once.

Or

If you wish to erase the text that is to the right side of the cursor, follow these steps:

- Erase characters by using the Backspace key once.
- Simply choose the text you want to erase from your document and press the delete key.
- Use the Delete or Backspace key to delete the current character.

4.3 Format Characters & Paragraphs

If you use text placeholders in your presentation, the template you choose will determine how you align and space the paragraphs. Paragraph formatting allows you to alter these and other aspects of a single paragraph. Selecting a paragraph with a click anywhere in it makes the options in a Paragraph group of the Home tab available for editing.

Character formatting allows you to change the appearance of individual words in addition to modifying the appearance of whole paragraphs. The commands in the Font group on the Home tab are used to make modifications after choosing the characters to format.

When you choose text in PowerPoint, the Mini Toolbar appears so you may quickly and easily style common paragraphs and characters. Next to the selected text is a toolbar with shortcuts to the options found in the Home tab's Font and Paragraph groups. If you don't want to utilize any of the Mini Toolbar's preset formats, you may dismiss it and make your own adjustments using the ribbon.

Line breaks may be modified after the text has been formatted on a slide to provide a more pleasing visual effect. The titles of slides are especially prone to needing line breaks, but even typical content like bullet points might occasionally benefit from having them added by hand.

To apply character attributes to text

Pick out the text you wish to format, and then use one of these methods:

To emphasize text, use the Bold, Underline, Italic, or Text Shadow and Strikethrough buttons in the Font group on the Home tab.

To apply a similar style, use one of the buttons found on the Mini Toolbar.

Make use of any of these shortcuts on your keyboard:

- Simply pressing Ctrl+B will make the currently highlighted text bold.
- Select the text you want to make italic and hit the Ctrl key plus the I key.
- Select the text you want to underline, then hit the Ctrl key and the U key at the same time.

To change text casing

Navigate to the Home tab, then the Font group, and finally, the Change Case button.

Aa ▾
Sentence case.
lowercase
UPPERCASE
Capitalize Each Word
tOGGLE cASE

Adjust the intercharacter spacing up or down.

First, under the Font section, choose the Character Spacing option and then either:

- Choose the desired spacing by clicking on it.
- The Font dialogue box's Character Spacing page may be accessed through the More Spacing button; once there, you can enter the desired amount of spacing between individual characters.

To alter the current text's font color

- Formatting text is to highlight it for editing.
- To change the font color, go to the Fonts section of the Home tab and click the arrow next to the desired color.
- Select a color from the Standard Colors palette.
- For enlarging the font size of preexisting text is to highlight that content.

Just two things to try:

- To make the text larger, choose the Font menu and then the Expand Font option.
- To do this, use Ctrl+Shift+>.
- In order to remove any text formatting
- To begin formatting, first, highlight the text you wish to change.

Take one of the two options below:

- To do this, open the Fonts panel and choose the Clear All Formatting option.
- For starters, use the Shift Spacebar combination.

To convert bulleted list items to regular text paragraphs

To convert the items in the bulleted list, click the things you wish to change.

Choose one of the two options below:

- To use bullet points, choose the active button in a Paragraph group on the Home tab.
- To disable the bullets in the gallery, choose that option from the drop-down menu.

It's easy to go from bulleted to numbered or numbered to bulleted format with only a few clicks.

To create a bulleted or numbered list

- Choose the things you want to include and then click the corresponding option.

Modify the bullet point or numerical format.

- Select the desired format by clicking the arrow next to Bullets or Numbering.

To change the alignment of text

Select one of the following alignment options in the Paragraph group on the Home tab:

- Click the Align Left button to have the text line up with the left side of the placeholder.
- To center the text in the placeholder, click the Center button.
- Using the Align Right option, you may have your text flush with the right side of the placeholder.
- With the Justify option selected, the text will be aligned to the left and right

margins, with sufficient white space between words to fill the line. (This choice is available if the paragraph has many lines.)
- Click the Align Text button to vertically center, align, or justify text in the placeholder.

Or

Make use of any one of these shortcuts on your keyboard:
- You may use Ctrl+L to align text to the left.
- Press Ctrl+E to align text in the middle of the screen.
- To right-align text, use the shortcut Ctrl+R.

Altering line spacing
- You may set the line spacing for your document by clicking the Line Spacing button in the Paragraph group of the Home tab.
- Using the Paragraph dialogue box's settings to style a paragraph
- Navigate to the Home tab and click the Paragraph dialogue box launcher to access the Paragraph dialogue box.

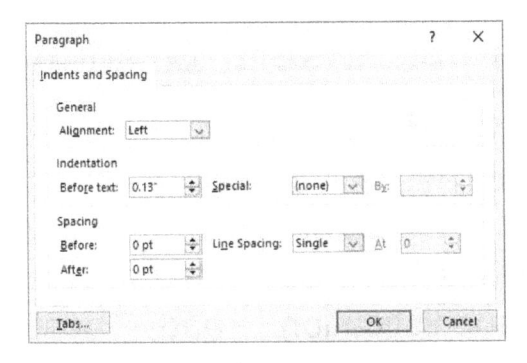

Take any of these actions:

- Adjust the Alignment to Left, Center, or Right in the General section.
- Put a number in the Before or After box under Spacing.
- You may adjust the line spacing by going to the Spacing menu.

First, use Shift+Enter to create a new line in the text.

Chapter 5: Insert & Manage Images & Graphics

Thanks to easily accessible, pre-made templates created by experts, presentations have advanced in terms of visual sophistication and aesthetic appeal. Presenters should no longer (ideally) just read out a list of bullet points; instead, effective presentations will likely have shorter words and more visual components. Visual aids such as photos, animations, tables, charts, and diagrams may help back up what you say verbally.

Photos, "clip art" pictures, graphs, charts, and geometrical forms are all examples of graphics. All of these visuals may be included as objects on the slide and then resized, moved, or copied. PowerPoint slides make it easier to communicate information creatively than Word documents can since slide components may float on their own.

Inserting, resizing, and repositioning images, editing and formatting images, drawing and manipulating shapes, recording and including screen clips, and making a photo album are all covered in this chapter.

5.1 Insert, Move & Resize Pictures

Slides in your PowerPoint 2023 presentations may include digital pictures as well as images made and stored in other applications. We refer to all of these individual photos as "pictures," for short. Slides may be made more visually attractive with the use of photos; however, in a PowerPoint presentation, the primary purpose of pictures is to communicate information that words alone can't.

A photograph may be added to a slide presentation from your local computer, the Internet, or a cloud storage service. Once an image has been included, it may be resized and moved about the slide to better suit your needs.

When you insert or choose an image, the Picture Tools tab group's Format tool tab appears, giving you access to the image's resizable handles. On this tab, you'll find options for adjusting an image's look and positioning in relation to the page's content and other pictures.

To insert a picture from your computer

Choose one of the following options to display the Insert Picture dialogue box:

- If the slide has a placeholder for content, choose the Pictures button from the placeholder.
- If the slide does not have a content placeholder, click the Pictures button in the Images group on the Insert tab.

In the Insert Picture dialogue box, go to and choose the image(s) to be inserted. Select the Insert button, then.

The image is enclosed by a frame to signify that it has been chosen. You may resize and rotate the image using the handles around the frame.

To insert a picture from an online source

Choose one of the following options to launch the Insert Images window:

- If the slide has a placeholder for content, click Online Pictures in the placeholder.

- If the slide does not have a contents placeholder, click on the Online Pictures button in the Images group on the Insert tab.

In the Insert Pictures window, pick the desired source or enter a search word in the search field.

Navigate to and choose the image to be inserted. Click the Insert button.

To select a picture for editing

- Click on the image once.

To relocate an image

- Indicate the picture. When a four-headed arrow appears as the cursor, drag the image to its new spot.

To resize an image

- Select the image and then do one of the below actions:
- To modify merely the image's width, drag the left or right size handle.
- To modify the image's height solely, move the top or bottom size handle.
- To modify the height and width of an image without affecting its aspect ratio, drag a corner size handle or adjust the Height or Width dimension

in the Group size on the Format tool tab, and then hit the Enter key.

Graphic formats

Many popular graphic formats save images as a collection of dots or pixels. Each pixel is composed of bits. The amount of bits per pixel (bpp) governs the number of unique colors that a pixel may represent.

The bit-to-color mapping is not 1:1; it is 2bpp. In other terms, one bpp equals two colors.

2 bits per pixel = 4 colors

4 bit per pixel = 16 colors

8 bits per colour = 256 colors

16 bits per pixel = 65,536 colors

5.2 Edit & Format Pictures

Throughout this book, we have referred to the recent tendency away from bullet-pointed slides and toward presentations with more visuals. Successful presenters have learned that the majority of audience members cannot listen to a presentation while reading the slides. Therefore, these presenters ensure that the majority of their slides have images that illustrate their message, providing the audience with anything to look at while they concentrate on what is being spoken. PowerPoint provides the tools necessary to build presentations that emphasize visuals over words.

Using the instructions on the Format tool tab, you may alter any image you include in a presentation. You may, for instance, perform the following:

- Remove the backdrop by selecting the parts you want to retain and those you wish to delete.
- Adjust the image's sharpness or softness, as well as its brightness and contrast.
- Enhance the color of the image.
- Make one of the hues in the image translucent.
- Select an effect like Pencil Sketch or Paint Strokes.
- Apply shadows, reflections, borders, or a mix of these effects.
- Add a border consisting of any number of solid or dashed lines of any width and color.

- You may rotate the image to any angle by sliding the turning handle or by selecting the rotate or flip option.
- Remove off the slide the portions of the image that you do not want to display. (The image is not changed; just portions of it are obscured.)
- Specify the optimal resolution for where or how a presentation will be seen, such as on a website or printed page, to reduce the presentation's file size. You may also remove the cropped portions of an image to lower its file size.
- All of these modifications are done to the image's representation on the slide and have no effect on the original image.

To crop a picture

- Select the image first. Click the Crop button in the Size group on the Format tool tab to show thick black handles on the image's edges and corners.
- Drag the handles to create the desired cropping area. The parts that will not be included in the cropped image are indicated by shading.

To frame a picture

- Choose the image. Click the More button in a Picture Styles group on the Format tool tab to view the Picture Styles gallery.

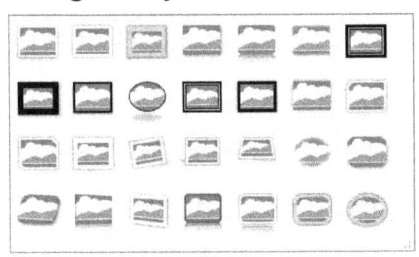

- Point successively to each photo style to observe a live preview of the frame applied to your image. Click the desired image style to apply it.
- To erase a picture's backdrop.
- Select the image first. Click the Remove Background button in the Adjust group of the Format tool tab to open the Background Removal tool tab and add a purple tint to the portions of the image that the tool believes you want to remove.
- Move the white handles to designate the area you want to retain. The Background Removal instrument refreshes its shade in real-time.

- On the Background Removal tool's tab, select Mark Areas to Keep, and then click any darkened portions of the image that you want to expose and retain.
- Select Mark Sections to Eliminate on a Background Removal tool's Mark Areas to Remove tab, and then click any non-shaded areas of the image that you want to remove.
- Depending on the simplicity of the image, you may need to make several or a few tweaks.

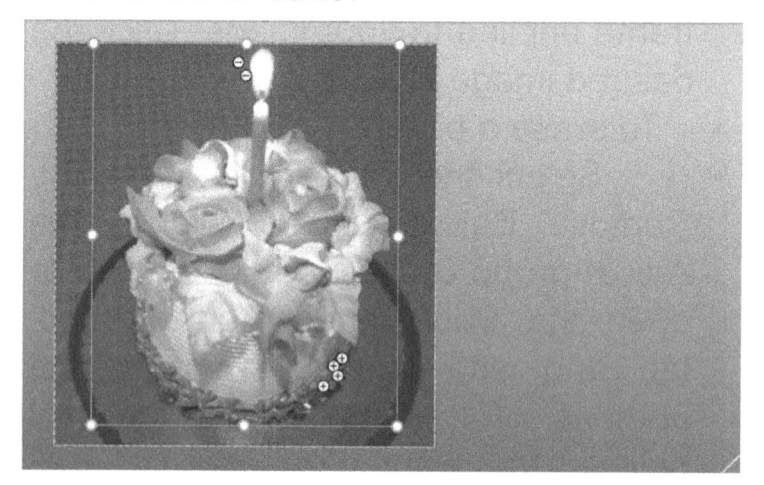

When you are finished, click the Save button to see the results. At any moment, you may return to the Background Removal tool tab to make modifications.

5.3 Create Charts

You may quickly add a chart to a presentation to assist in identifying patterns that may not be apparent from the statistics alone. PowerPoint 2023 has 15 chart types, including Combo graphs, which show several data series separately on a single axis.

These are the most common chart categories:

- **Column** These graphs illustrate how values fluctuate over time.
- **Line** These graphs depict numbers that fluctuate erratically over time.
- **Pie** These diagrams illustrate the relationship between the parts and the whole.
- **Bar** These graphs depict the values of many variables at a given moment.

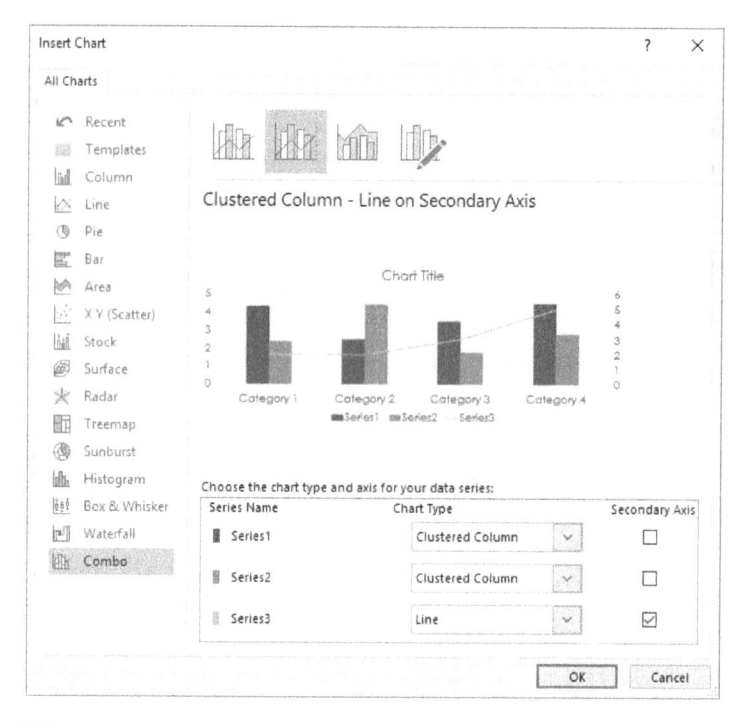

There are two-dimensional and three-dimensional variants of some chart types. Office 2023 adds the Treemap, histogram, Sunburst, Box & Whisker, and Waterfall sections to the Microsoft Office programs.

PowerPoint creates a connected Microsoft Excel spreadsheet with example data that corresponds to the chosen chart type when you build a chart. You change the example data in the spreadsheet with your own data, and a chart on the slide adjusts to represent your data.

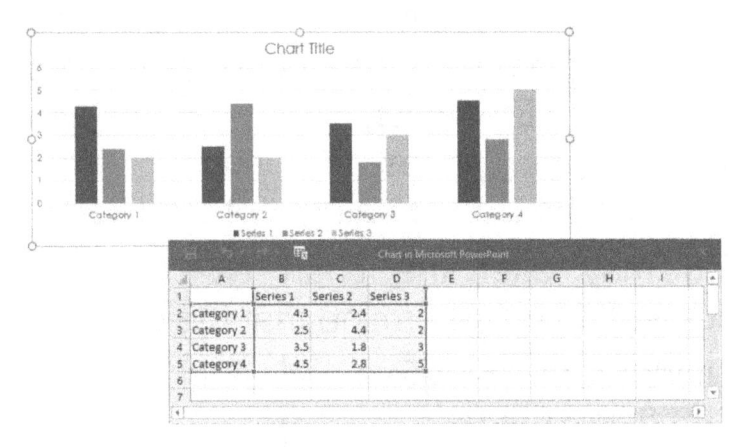

You may either manually input the data into the connected spreadsheet or copy and paste it into an existing Microsoft Access table, Excel worksheet or Word table.

After plotting the data in a chart, you may reposition and resize the chart to match the available space on the slide, as well as add or delete chart components to define the chart's content most clearly for the audience. You may modify the worksheet's data at any moment, including the values and column and row titles.

PowerPoint redraws the graph to reflect your modifications.

When a graph is active on a slide, you may manipulate the chart and its components using the Format and Design tool tabs on the ribbon, as well as the Chart Elements, chart filters and Chart Styles, panes that appear when you click the icons to a right of the chart.

You may alter the chart type at any moment if you determine that the one you originally chose does not appropriately represent your data.

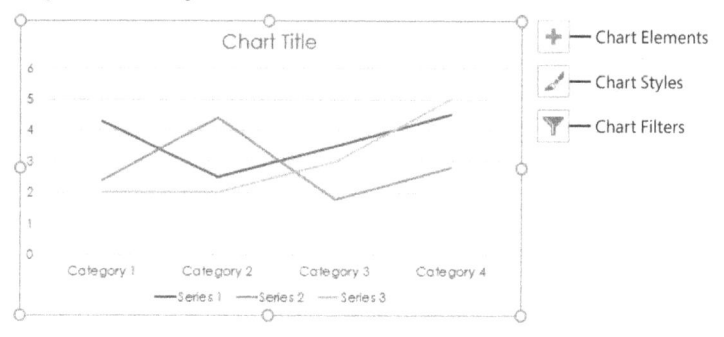

To create a chart on a slide

Follow one of the steps below to launch the Insert Chart dialogue box:

- In a placeholder for content, click the Insert Chart button.
- In the Illustrations category of the Insert tab, click the Chart button.

Clicking a chart category in the left pane of an Insert Chart dialogue box displays the chart variants in the right pane.

2. Click the chart type you want to create in the right pane, and then click OK to insert an example chart and open the related Excel spreadsheet containing the plotted data.

3. Enter the numbers to be plotted in the attached Excel spreadsheet, following the format of the example data.

If a chart data range specified by the colorful outlines does not immediately extend to incorporate new data, drag a blue handle in the range's lower-right corner to expand it.

Close the Microsoft Excel window.

To insert a chart from Excel onto a slide

- Click the chart's border in the source worksheet to choose it.
- Copy the diagram to the Clipboard.
- Display the presentation in PowerPoint and then paste a chart from a Clipboard.

To change the type of a selected chart

1. Click a Change Chart Type button in the Type category on the Design tool tab.
2. In a Change Chart Type dialogue box, pick a category on the left, then click a chart type at the top.

Chapter 6: Finalize Presentation

In the past, presenters made presentations with limited supporting resources. Gradually, "visual aids" such as whiteboard drawings and easel-mounted flip charts were incorporated. Eventually, clever presenters started projecting 35mm slides or transparencies onto screens alongside their speeches. Early versions of PowerPoint provided output formats suited for slides of different sizes, including 35mm slides and also the acetate sheets used with overhead projectors to accommodate these speakers.

As a result of technological advancements, the majority of presentations are now provided online. When you create a new presentation using the Blank Presentation template or any of the PowerPoint design templates, the slides are formatted for a widescreen monitor. This is because it is likely that you will deliver the presentation using a portable computer and a projection device optimized for this format. By default, slides are horizontally orientated with a width-to-height ratio of 16:9 and real measurements of 13.333 by 7.5 inches.

6.1 Configure Slides For Presentation Or Printing

If you find it essential to adjust the size of a presentation's slides to match the display you're using, you may do so effortlessly. Keep in mind, though, that you will need to inspect the slides carefully to verify that the original information still fits. PowerPoint invites you to decide whether you want to maximize the size of the slide content or scale it down to guarantee it fits when you reduce the height or width of a slide.

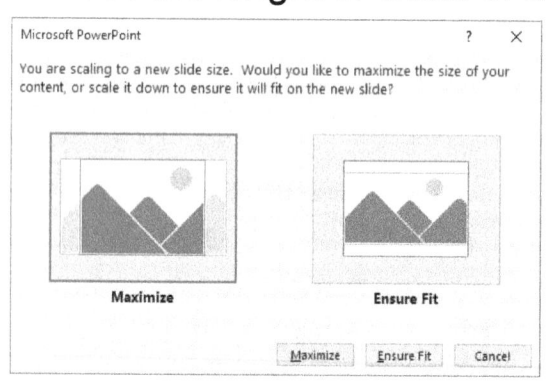

Only "live" slide material is affected by the content scaling option. Changing the slide size may compress or stretch pictures that are parts of the slide layout, such as background images or logos, regardless of the content scaling option you choose. Change the Scale Width option for the impacted photos on the slide layouts to resolve the issue.

If the Widescreen and Standard formats do not meet your requirements — for instance, if you wish to size the slides to match a specified paper size for printing — you may click Custom Slide Size at the bottom of the Slide Size menu and choose from the following slide sizes in the Slide Size dialogue box:

On-screen Display (4:3) For an electronic slide presentation on a variety of screens: 4:3 (format Standard), 16:9 (format Widescreen), or 16:10 (format Widescreen).

For a presentation that will be printed on letter-sized paper measuring 8.5 by 11 inches.

For a presentation that will be printed on legal-size paper measuring 11 by 17 inches.

A3 Paper, B4 (ISO), A4 Paper, and B5 Paper (ISO) Paper are needed for presentations which will be printed on paper sizes across the globe.

35mm Slides needed 35mm slides that will be exhibited using a slide projector using a slide carousel.

Overhead For overhead projector-displayed transparency slides.

Banner For website banner images.

For slides with non-standard dimensions. In a Slide Size dialogue box, you may specify the height, width, and orientation of the slide.

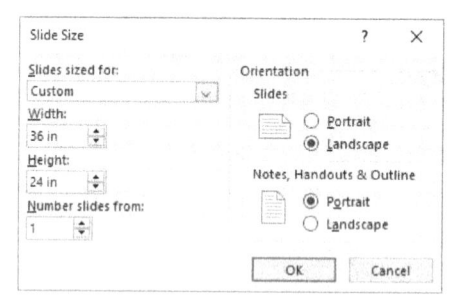

```
Slide Size                                    ?    X

Slides sized for:              Orientation
  Custom            v            Slides
Width:                             O Portrait
  36 in    ↕                       ● Landscape
Height:
  24 in    ↕                    Notes, Handouts & Outline
Number slides from:                ● Portrait
  1        ↕                       O Landscape

                              OK          Cancel
```

To set the slide size to a standard screen aspect ratio

On the Design tab, under the Customize group, select the Slide Size button, followed by one of the options below:

- Click Standard to adjust the aspect ratio of a slide to 4:3 (4:3).
- To adjust the aspect ratio of a slide to 16:9, choose Widescreen (16:9).
- Click Custom Slide Size to tailor the slides for a non-standard screen aspect ratio or paper size.

PowerPoint allows you to indicate how you wish to alter the slide's content if your option reduces the slide's height or width. Choose to Maximize in a Microsoft PowerPoint dialogue box to retain text and graphics as big as feasible, or click Ensure Fit to scale the whole slide's content.

To adjust the size of the slide to the regular print size or screen aspect ratio

- Click a Slide Size button, followed by Custom Slide Size, on the Design tab's Customize group.

In the Dialogue Box for Slide Size, do the following:

- Select the proper screen aspect ratio or paper size or from a Slides sized for the pull-down option.

- Select the appropriate slide orientation by clicking Landscape or portrait in the Slides box inside the Orientation section.
- Click Accept.
- If your selection lowers the height or width of the presentation, PowerPoint will prompt you to modify the slide's content. Select Maximize in a Microsoft PowerPoint dialogue box to maintain text and images at their largest possible size, or select Ensure Fit to scale the whole slide's content.

To set a custom slide size

- In the Customize group on the Design tab, select the Slide Size option, followed by Custom Slide Size.

In the Dialogue Box for Slide Size, do the following:

- Click Custom in the Slides sized for the list.
- Adjust the Width and Height to your liking. If the width is less than the height, the slide orientation defaults to Portrait; if the width is higher than the height, it defaults to Landscape.

- To swap the dimensions for Width and Height, click the other orientation in the Slides area of the Orientation section.
- Select OK.

PowerPoint allows you to indicate how you wish to alter the slide's content if your option reduces the slide's height or width. Choose to Maximize in the Microsoft PowerPoint dialogue box to retain text and graphics as big as feasible, or click Ensure Fit to scale the whole slide's content.

To scale slide layout images

- Display the presentations in Slide Master view and identify a slide layout with an improperly sized picture.
- Select a picture by clicking on it. Click the Size dialogue box launcher on the Format tool tab to reveal the Properties and sizes page of the Format Picture pane.

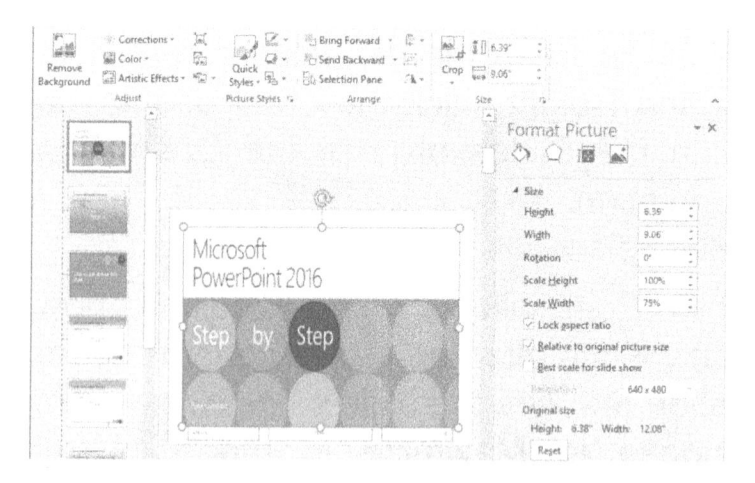

Review the settings for Scale Height and Scale Width. Change the bigger number to correspond with the smaller number, and then resize the picture to meet the new slide size.

6.2 Print Presentations & Handouts

The majority of this book is devoted to the design of slide shows for the on-screen delivery of presentations. PowerPoint also allows for the printing of presentations, either as slides or as handouts with slides and notes. You may print a presentation for evaluation or for dissemination to other individuals.

When printing a presentation, you may choose from a variety of slide and handout formats. You may preview the presentation as it will look when printed and adjust the print parameters to your specifications. All of these operations are performed on the Print page of the Backstage view.

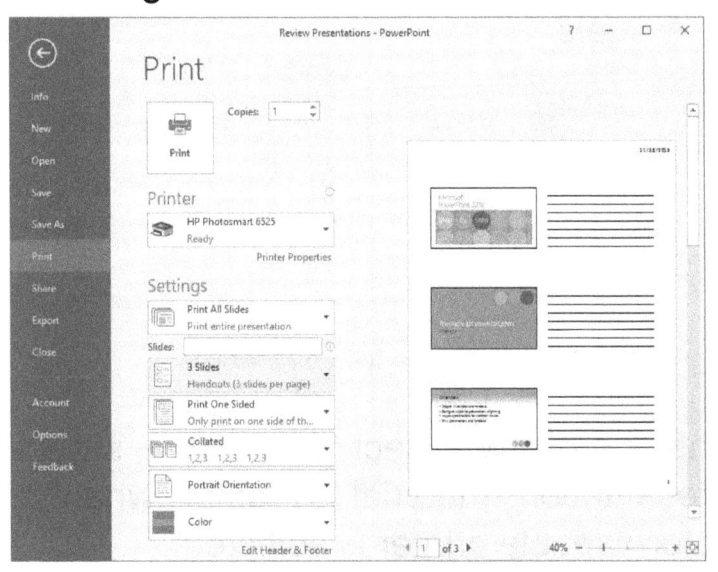

Choosing a printer and adjusting the print settings is an easy procedure. Here is what you have to know about printing with PowerPoint compared to other applications:

- You may choose to print the complete presentation or individual slides.

- You may print between one and nine slides per paper, as well as handouts that contain slides, slide notes, and room for taking notes. If you just need the text of slides, you may print the presentation's outline without the visuals.

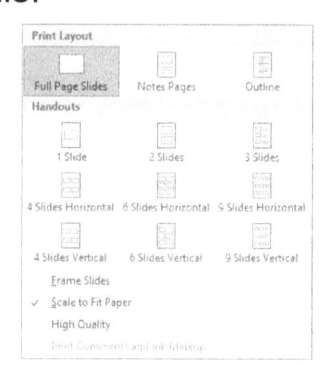

The preview section only shows presentation material in color when a color-capable printer is selected.

You may choose Grayscale, Color or Pure Black and White for the output and preview. If the chosen printer is not a color printer, choosing Color shows the presentation as it would look if PowerPoint transmitted it to the printer in a color format as opposed to grayscale or black-and-white.

Even when the Pure Black & White option is selected, some items will print in grayscale. The following table describes how particular things will appear when printing in grayscale or clear black and white.

Object	Grayscale	Pure Black And White
Text	Black	Black
Bitmaps	Grayscale	Grayscale
Charts	Grayscale	Grayscale
Clip art	Grayscale	Grayscale
Embossing	Grayscale	Hidden
Fills	Grayscale	White
Frames	Black	Black
Lines	Black	Black
Object shadows	Grayscale	Black
Pattern fills	Grayscale	White
Slide backgrounds	White	White
Text shadows	Grayscale	Hidden

If you want to enhance the information on the prints, you may add headers and footers, including the page numbers, date and time or any other information you choose to print on each page.

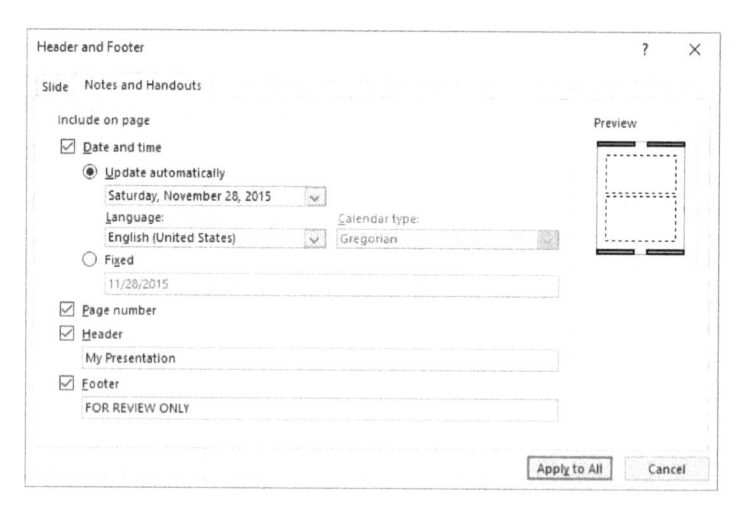

In lieu of printing the handouts using the print options, you have the option to export the presentation material to a Word file in which you might hypothetically develop the pages further.

Select the slide or slides to print

- If just one slide is to be printed, show that slide. Select the desired slides in a Thumbnails pane of Normal view or Slide Sorter view to print them.
- Display the Print page in Backstage mode.

Under the Settings area, open the first list, and then perform one of the following in the Slides section:

- To print the full presentation, choose Print All Slides from the menu.

- To print just the slides that are presently chosen, click Print Selection.
- Click Print Current Slide to print just the currently shown slide.
- To pick certain slides by providing a custom range, click Custom Range and then enter slide figures separated by commas, ranges divided by hyphens, or both in the Slides box. (For instance, typing 2,5,12-15 in the Slides box will print slides 2, 5, 12, 13, and 15).

Select the print format

In the Settings section of the Print page of the Backstage view, open the second menu and then choose one of the following options:
- Click Full Page Slides to print one slide per page with no further material.
- Click Notes Pages to print one slide per page with the slide notes below the slide.
- Click Outline to print a text outline of the slide's content.

To print handouts, under the Handouts area of the menu, select the thumbnail that corresponds to the number and sequence of slides you want to print per page. The horizontal orientation sorts the slides from left to the right and then from top to bottom, while the vertical orientation sorts the slides from top to bottom and then from left to right. If uncertain, choose an option to preview it.

Click Frame Slides to add or remove the frame around each picture. A checked box indicates that the option is enabled.

To print double-sided pages

- In the Settings section of the Print page in the Backstage view, open the third menu, and then select the Print on Both Sides thumbnail that corresponds to the desired page flipping direction.

To preview the printouts

The preview box will only show you the slides that you have chosen to print, formatted in the manner that you have chosen. You may get a preview of the content of the printing by doing any of the following:

- To proceed to the next or previous page of a printout, click the Next Page

or Previous Page button that is located below the lower-left corner of the preview. Alternatively, you may use the arrows to navigate among the pages.
- To go to a particular page in the printout, enter the page number in the box that is located below the lower-left corner of the preview, and then hit the Enter key on your keyboard.
- To navigate through the pages that will be printed, either move the scroll bar with your mouse or click either the top or bottom of the scroll box.
- Clicking the Zoom to Page button located in the lower-right-hand corner of the Print page will cause the page to be shown at the biggest size that will still fit in the preview window.
- You may adjust the size of the page by dragging the Zoom slider or clicking the Zoom In or Zoom Out buttons, respectively.

To specify the print colors
- While in the Backstage view, go to the Print page and choose the printer that you want to use. This will let

PowerPoint know whether or not the printer supports color printing.

In the box labeled Settings, choose Color, and then select one of the following options:

- When printing, choose Color from the drop-down menu to provide the color settings.
- Select the Grayscale option in the drop-down menu to convert colors to different tones of grey.
- Click the Pure Black and White button to convert any colors to black or white, with the exception of those found in charts, bitmaps, and clip art images.

To add headers or footers to printouts

To see the Notes and Handouts page in the Header and Footer dialogue box, do one of the following steps:

- In the Backstage view, open the Print page and display it. To edit the header and footer, click the link that is located at the bottom of the center pane.

- Make sure the presentation is shown using the Notes Page view. Click the Header & Footer button that is located in the Text group under the Insert tab in Microsoft Word.

Carry out one of the following actions:

- Check the box labeled Date and time, then click the OK button. Select Fixed, and then input the date and time in the format that you want to show them in. Alternatively, you may pick Update automatically and then click the format that you want to display the date and time in.
- Check the box designated for the page number.
- First, make sure the Header check box is selected, and then, in the following box, type the text that you would want to appear at the very top of the page.
- First, select the box labeled "Footer," and then, in the space provided for it, type the content that you wish to appear at the very bottom of the page.

Hit the "Apply to All" button.

To export handouts to Word

1. The Export section of the Backstage view should be shown.
2. To open a Send To Microsoft Word dialogue box, click the Create Handouts button in the center pane and then click the Create Handouts button in the right pane.

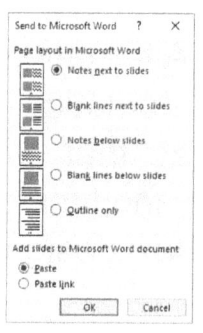

1. In the section of the dialogue box designated for Page layout in Microsoft Word, click the page layout that you wish to use.
2. In the section designated for adding slides to a document in Microsoft Word, you may do either of the following:

- Click the Paste button in order to include the slides in the document without preserving a connection to the presentation.
- Click the Paste link button to embed and link slides in the document, allowing you to simply edit the document to reflect any changes made to the presentation.

   3. Depress the "OK" button. Word will initiate and complete the creation of the handout, notes page, or outline that you choose. You are free to make any further modifications to the Word document that you see fit, as well as add new comments.

6.3 10 Essential Formulas Requested by a Company

As a public speaker, there is nothing more terrifying than knowing that your audience is dozing off. To avoid it from occurring, consider these options.

Don't Forget Your Purpose

Way too many speakers drone on and on without ever getting to the point. There's pressure to include every funny anecdote and the amusing fact you can think of that has anything to do with your presentation's theme. The inability to define your presentation's purpose will make resisting this temptation difficult. Put differently; you haven't identified your true motivation.

Don't get the presentation's title mixed up with what it's really about. Let's say you're the one who will be pitching your company's new and enhanced deluxe model Chron Sim plastics in findibulator to a potential customer. This presentation isn't meant to enlighten the customer about the new Infindibulator; rather, it's meant to sell them on purchasing one of these monstrosities at the cost of $65 million. Even if your presentation is titled "Infindibulators for the 21st Century," your true goal is to "Convince these saps to purchase one, or maybe two."

Be careful, and do not let your slides control you.

The presentations that may be created using PowerPoint are so well designed that there is a strong temptation to let them take center stage. That's a tremendous error. You, not the slides, are the main attraction here. The slides are only visual aids that are meant to make your presentation more successful. They are not intended to take the spotlight away from you.

Your slides should be a complement to your discussion rather than a repetition of what you just said. If you discover that you are just reading the slides, you may want to reconsider what you have included on the slides. Instead of serving as a script for your presentation, the slides should provide a summary of the essential topics.

Do not Overwhelm Your Readers with Extraneous Information

Edward Everett was considered to be one of the best orators of his day, and on November 19, 1863, a throng of 15,000 people assembled at Gettysburg to hear him speak. Mr. Everett gave a talk that lasted for two hours about the legendary conflict and the events that had taken place throughout it. Abraham Lincoln stood up after he had done speaking to give a quick two-minute postscript that went on to become the most famous speech in the history of the United States.

Everett most likely would have delivered a presentation that lasted for four hours if PowerPoint had been available back in 1863. PowerPoint encourages you to speak too much by its very nature. When you start typing bullets, you won't be able to stop until you finish. You'll soon have forty slides for a presentation that only lasts twenty minutes. There are roughly 35 more than what is probably required of you there. During your presentation, you should aim to show one slide every two to five minutes.

You Should Not Ignore Your Opening

They say that you only have one chance to create a first impression, and you need to make it count. Do not throw away this opportunity by cracking a joke that has no connection with the subject matter, apologizing for your lack of preparation or anxiousness, or reciting your credentials.

Don't beat about the bush; just get to the heart of the matter.

The most effective beginnings are those that immediately grab the attention of the audience by means of a thought-provoking remark, a rhetorical question, or an engaging anecdote. It's OK to open with a joke, but only if it does anything to establish the tone for what your presentation will be about.

Be Relevant

The objective of every presentation should be to get the audience to agree with you and say, "Me too!" Sadly, many presentations leave an audience with the question, "So what?"

It is imperative that you provide the people of your audience with what they need rather than focusing on what you consider to be fascinating or significant. Rather than presenting ideas on fictitious issues, the most convincing arguments are those that give answers to actual problems.

Do not forget to make a Call to Action

What use would a sales presentation serve if there was never an attempt to close the deal? An opportunity that was not taken.

The most effective presentations are the ones in which the audience is prompted to take some kind of action. This might mean that they make a purchase from you, alter how they live their lives, or just become interested enough in the subject at hand to read more about it. The chance, however, will be lost on you if you do not in some manner ask your audience to react to what you have said.

Make it very obvious to your audience how they may purchase whatever it is that you are offering (and we are all marketing something!). Give them the number that doesn't cost them anything. Provide them with a handout that includes connections to websites that they may visit to get further information. You should all take turns singing "Just As I Am." Do whatever it takes to get it done.

Practice, Practice, Practice

Here we go again with good old Abe: There is a persistent urban legend circulating that Abraham Lincoln hurriedly penned the Gettysburg Address aboard the train just as it was about to pull into the station at Gettysburg. In point of fact, Lincoln stewed over each and every phrase for many agonizing weeks.

Strive to get through the difficult parts. Polish both the beginning and the end, as well as any uncomfortable transitions that may have occurred in between. Perform your exercises in front of the mirror. Make a video of yourself. Keep track of the time. Practice.

Relax!

Don't be concerned! Enjoy yourselves! Every time they take the stage in front of an audience, even the best public speakers have butterflies in their stomachs. Relax no matter who you are talking to, whether it's one person or ten thousand. In twenty minutes, everything will be finished.

No one except you is aware of how anxious you feel, and even then, only if you choose to share that information with them. Never apologize for the things you're afraid of; this is the first and most important guideline for avoiding panic attacks. When you are behind the podium, no one will see if your knees are hitting together violently enough to give you a bruise since no one else can see them. People will ask you, "Weren't you nervous? " after they have finished swabbing down your underarm and wiping the drool off of your chin. You seemed to be really calm.

Be prepared for the unexpected.

Prepare yourself for the fact that things will go wrong because they will. It is possible that the projector will not focus, that the microphone will stop working, and that you will lose your notes on the way to the platform. Who can predict what else could take place?

Take everything in stride, but do your best to foresee potential challenges and prepare for them. Keep an additional set of notes in the pocket of your pants. If you have a microphone of your own, please bring it with you. If at all feasible, you should have a second projector available. Bring 2 copies of your presentation on flash drives, but be sure to keep them separate from one another in your briefcase.

Don't Be Boring

An audience is able to forgive practically everything, but if you bore them, there is one thing you will never be forgiven for. Above all, do not bore your audience.

This recommendation does not imply that you are required to make jokes, hop up and down, or speak very quickly. Inconceivably dull activities include making jokes, dancing around excessively, and speaking very quickly. If you follow the other directions in this book — if you have a well-defined goal and remain committed to that mission, if you steer clear of needless detail, and if you focus on meeting actual needs — you will never be boring. Simply be yourself and enjoy the ride. If you're having a good time, your audience will, too.

Conclusion

PowerPoint is the industry standard for presentations, whether they are for conferences, businesses, or schools. The program allows anybody who wants to communicate properly to produce effective slideshow displays that include information in the form of graphs, clipart, sound, and video. The fundamental knowledge and skills you have to master Microsoft PowerPoint are revealed in PowerPoint, which is jam-packed with practical guidance and step-by-step instructions.

PowerPoint presentations may be an effective method to deliver information in bite-sized chunks. Bullet points, photos, tables, charts, and business diagrams may all be included on individual slides. Themes that have been professionally developed aesthetically improve your message and offer a professional, cohesive look.

The user interface refers to the aspects that influence the look of PowerPoint and how you interface with it when creating presentations. Some user interface aspects are just ornamental, such as the color scheme. Others, such as menus, toolbars and buttons, are useful. The default PowerPoint setup and functionality are based on how the majority of users use the software. You may change the appearance and functionality of user interface components to fit your tastes and working style.

This book walks you through the steps of generating presentations, opening and browsing presentations, showing various presentation views, displaying and altering presentation attributes, and saving and terminating presentations.